Process Kaizen

How to Document and Improve Any Process (and everything's a process...)

Philip Kling

Copyright © 2012 Philip Kling

All rights reserved.

ISBN: 1479306290
ISBN-13: 978-1479306299

DEDICATION

For my mother, who inspired me to think and to feel.

Process Kaizen

Table of Contents

Acknowledgements 11

The Purpose of this Book 13

A Quick Refresher on Lean and Kaizen Events 15

Understanding Lean Thinking 20

Understanding Six Sigma 21

Understanding 6S (AKA 5S, 5S+1) 22

Understanding Visual Controls and Management with Kanban 25

Understanding Pull Systems and One Piece Flow 26

Understanding the DMAIC Methodology 28

The Kaizen Event Process 32

1. Identify Opportunity 34

1.01 Identify Strategic Goals 35

    Figure 1.01.01 - Understanding Kaizen Opportunities 36

    Figure 1.01.02 - Strategic Objectives Discovery Template 40

1.02 Determine Measure(s) and Baseline 42

    Figure 1.02.01 – Understanding Primary Metrics 43

    Figure 1.02.02 - Collecting Baseline Data 45

1.03 Identify Variance in Performance to Plan 50

1.04 Stakeholder Submits Idea 52

    Figure 1.04.01 Making Ideas Visible 53

    Figure 1.04.02 Identifying Opportunities through an Andon Cord System 55

    Andon Cord: Traditional Examples 56

    Andon Cord: Office Examples 57

1.05 Facilitate Organizational Assessment 58

    Figure 1.05.01 – Lean Organization Assessment Example 59

    Figure 1.05.02 – 6S Audit Examples 64

1.06 Establish Baseline Performance 67
    Figure 1.06.01 Understanding Baseline Performance Reports 68
1.07 Prioritize Opportunities 71
Figure 1.07.01 – Prioritizing Kaizen Opportunities 73
2. Charter Project...78
2.01 Collect/Review Baseline Performance Data 79
2.02 Quantify Performance and Financial Impacts 80
    Figure 2.02.01 – Determining Process Capability 81
2.03 Identify Project Objectives..83
    Figure 2.03.01 – Example Kaizen Event Project Objectives..................84
2.04 Calculate Project Benefits 84
    Figure 2.04.01 – Understanding Charter Selection Criteria.................86
2.05 Draft Kaizen Charter..89
    Figure 2.05.01 - Understanding a Kaizen Project Charter 91
    Figure 2.05.02 – Kaizen Event Project Charter Template 92
2.06 Prioritize Kaizen Charters..94
    Figure 2.06.01 – Understanding Project Selection Criteria..................95
3. Kickoff Project..99
3.01 Identify Resources..100
3.02 Schedule Resources 101
    Figure 3.02.01 - Kaizen Event Team Directory Communication Sheet Template.102
3.03 Deep Dive Data for Categories of Failure Modes...............................102
    Figure 3.03.01 – Establishing Risk and Confidence Intervals 104
Figure 3.04.02 - Failure Modes Effects Analysis – Deep Dive Template 107
3.04 Facilitate Lean Thinking Exercise 108
    Figure 3.04.01 – Facilitating a Lean Thinking Exercise........................111
    Figure 3.04.02 – Lego Assembly Job Instruction Breakdown Sheets 115
3.05 Review Project Charter with Kaizen Team 118

4. Define Process 120

4.01 Review SIPOC Approach 121

    Figure 4.01.01 – Understanding the SIPOC 122

    Figure 4.01.02 - Example SIPOC 124

4.02 Develop SIPOC 126

    Figure 4.02.01 – SIPOC Template 128

4.03 Review Process Map Approach 130

    Figure 4.03.01 – Understanding Process Maps 131

4.04 Define Level 1 Process Map 133

    Figure 4.04.01 – Process Map Template 135

    Figure 4.04.02 – Process Level 1 Process Map Example 136

4.05 Define Sub-process Maps 136

    Figure 4.05.01 – Sub-process Map Example 137

4.06 Finalize Define Phase Process Maps 137

    Figure 4.06.01 – Process Map Standards 138

4.07 Draft Process Definition Document 140

    Figure 4.07.01 – Process Definition Document Template 141

    Figure 4.07.01 – Process Definition Document Example 142

5. Measure Process 143

5.01 Establish Level 1 Process Times and Lag Times 144

5.02 Determine Level 1 Primary Metric(s) 145

5.03 Estimate Sub-process Times and Lag Times 146

5.04 Determine Sub-process Primary Metric(s) 147

5.05 Review Value Added Flow Analysis Approach 147

    Figure 5.05.01 Understanding Value Added Flow Analysis 148

5.06 Perform Value Added Flow Analysis 151

5.07 Finalize Measure Phases Process Maps 152

5.08 Define Sub-process Activity Inputs and Outputs 153

6. Analyze Process 155

6.01 Prepare Cause and Effect Matrix 156

Figure 6.01.01 – Cause and Effect Matrix Template 157

6.02 Perform Cause and Effect Analysis 158

    Figure 6.02.01 – Understanding Cause and Effect Analysis 159

Figure 6.02.02 – Cause and Effect Matrix Example 160

6.03 Review Failure Modes Effect Analysis Approach 161

    Figure 6.03.01 – Understanding Failure Modes Effects Analysis 162

Figure 6.03.02 – Failure Modes Effects Analysis Template 164

Figure 6.03.03 – Failure Modes Effects Analysis Example 165

6.04 Perform Failure Modes Effects Analysis 165

6.05 Summarize Analysis and Review Improvement Recommendations 167

7. Improve Process 169

7.01 Update FMEA 170

7.02 Develop Improvement Backlog 171

    Figure 7.02.01 – Understanding Kaizen Event Improvement Backlogs ... 172

    Figure 7.02.02 – Kaizen Event Improvement Backlog Template 174

    Figure 7.02.03 – Kaizen Event Improvement Backlog Example 175

7.03 Plan Improvement Sprint Backlog 176

    Figure 7.03.01 – Understanding Improvement Planning 177

7.04 Complete Improvement Sprint Tasks 179

7.05 Review Improvement Sprint Results 180

7.06 Complete Improvement Sprint Retrospective 181

    Figure 7.06.01 Improvement Sprint Retrospective Template 182

Appendix: Implementing Lean Improvements 184

Standard Work 185

Training 190

Elimination of Wastes 192

- 6S Housekeeping and Organization ... 194
- Setup Reduction/Elimination ... 196
- What is Total Productive Maintenance? ... 199
- Visual Controls & Kanban ... 202
- TAKT Time ... 205
- Continuous Flow ... 209
- Just in Time ... 210
- Tracking and Reporting Progress and Performance Improvement ... 212
- Glossary of Terms ... 217

Process Kaizen

Acknowledgements

I am forever grateful to my wife and daughter. They are the critical factors of my life and I hope that I can always meet the upper specification limits for a good husband and father. Laura and Nova continuously support me in accomplishing my goals. Also, many thanks to the early readers, editors, and proofers. Specifically, thank you to Catherine Sheehy who eagerly consumed the early pages of the book and provided the most thoughtful and thorough feedback an author can receive. Thanks to Ben McDonald, Ed Thune, and Lisa Roullard for acting as incredible sounding boards and reality checkers. And thank you to all the people who have walked the Lean Journey with me. Our blood, sweat, and tears developed the structure of this process. And, once again, thanks to my wife Laura, who is an amazing partner and collaborator.

Process Kaizen

The Purpose of this Book

Process Kaizen is a quick and easy to use how-to guide and reference book designed to supplement and reinforce best practices and standard work for Kaizen Event facilitators and project team members. Thousands of Kaizen Event team members have utilized the information in this book to support their training, learning, implementation, and facilitation of Kaizen Events.

Process Kaizen is intended to assist continuous improvement professionals and leadership within the business areas of manufacturing, service, and knowledge-worker environments. Using the material in this book, any project team should be able to effectively scope the opportunity, engage the right people, and facilitate Kaizen Events with measurable results. The clear, concise presentations, process documentation, templates and examples allow beginners and experienced practitioners alike to succeed at implementing and facilitating Kaizen Events within any organization and targeting any process.

The purposes of this book are to:

1. Act as an easy to use Kaizen Event reference guide – usable by anyone and easy to understand at a glance
2. Act as a Kaizen Event Planner for any process and for any opportunity identified or problem encountered
3. Act as a single source of truth for learning the principles and completing the deliverables of Kaizen Events

Although not exhaustively comprehensive, Process Kaizen should enable readers to identify opportunities, baseline performance data, charter projects, plan and facilitate Kaizen Events, track benefits and report results.

You will find every Kaizen Event process, activity and deliverable broken out in detail so you have a clear understanding of the activities and deliverables. Examples are provided so you can see how each deliverable is completed and how they fit together to improve a process.

Process Kaizen

A Quick Refresher on Lean and Kaizen Events

A "Kaizen Organization" believes in the fundamental virtues of the basic Lean principles. Within a "Kaizen Organization", everyone is focused on identifying and eliminating sources of waste and inefficiency. Kaizen Organizations look at the world through the eyes of their customer and seek to fulfill customer expectations in a tangible and real way. They value only what the customer values.

Kaizen and Lean are NOT just applicable on the factory floor. In fact, there are considerably more opportunities in standard business operations than typical manufacturing processes. If you do not point Kaizen at regular business operations, you will most likely lose the transformative power of Lean and Kaizen and realize only a fraction of its potential. The true power of Kaizen lies in its inherent ability to unlock the potential of the entire organization. Kaizen Thinking can transform everything that an organization does.

The Hard and Soft Benefits of Kaizen

- Dramatic improvement in responsiveness to customers
    - Increased customer satisfaction
    - Reduced defects
    - Improved delivery
    - Increased market share
- Most of the production-floor chaos is eliminated
    - Eliminated batch production
    - 80-90% reduction in production flow times
    - No expedites needed for special orders
    - Re-work eliminated
    - Scrap significantly reduced
    - Factory floor is organized and clean
- Labor productivity is double or triple that of past
- Production control and information systems are greatly simplified
- Shipments from suppliers streamlined
- Storage space and associated inventory reduced by 80-90%
- Completed orders are shipped immediately

To support these claims, the book *Lean Thinking* (Womack and Jones 1996, p.27) reports the following improvements from converting to Lean:

Improvement Area	Initial Lean Transformation	Continuous Improvement
Labor Productivity	Double	Double Again
Production Throughput Times	90% Reduction	50% Reduction
Inventories (Throughout)	90% Reduction	50% Reduction
Errors Reaching Customers	50% Reduction	50% Reduction
Scrap	50% Reduction	50% Reduction
Time to Market for New Products	50% Reduction	50% Reduction

Values in the "Initial Lean Transformation" column are the results that can be expected from the initial conversion effort. Values in the "Continuous Improvement" column can be expected from continuous improvement efforts within 2-3 years. Improvements can be expected to continue indefinitely, but at a declining rate.

Lean thinking can and should be applied to ALL functions in the organization. Consider, for example, the Lean principle of "one piece flow." Here is how these principles could be implemented across several organizational functions.

Organizational Function	One Piece Flow Applied
Production	Parts and assemblies never stop moving until order is shipped
Product Design	Design never stops moving forward until it is in production
Business Processes	Paperwork (or electronic equivalent) never stops moving until processing is complete

The same Lean principles associated with material flow and processing can be applied to information flow and processing.

While it is fairly straightforward to quantify the benefits of Lean thinking within the production environment, it can be a significant challenge to determine the benefits of applying Lean thinking to business processes. Generally, you should be able to expect the following:

- "Voice of the Customer" becomes the driving force in the organization
- The workforce is empowered
- Decision making becomes decentralized
- Organizational structure shifts from vertical to a horizontal focus
- Responsiveness to changing market conditions is enhanced
- Relationships with suppliers and customers are revolutionized
- Continuously lower prices
- Improved operating margins and increased flexibility provide enhanced business opportunities

What would happen if your organization and its key suppliers mastered the application of Kaizen and Lean practices where they approached the level of a best in class practitioner of the methodology?

What could this look like at your organization?

- Cycle time down by 50%
- Product development man-hours down by 50%
- Software development costs down by 50%
- Prototypes made without tools
- No physical mockups
- Engineering changes after release reduced by 50%
- Paperwork virtually eliminated
- Assembly touch hours down by 50%
- Nonconformance costs down by 70%
- Assembly support labor down by 80%
- Inventory reduced by 90%
- Assembly cycle time down by 50%
- Engineering changes reduced by 60%
- Fabrication costs reduced by 50%
- Part lead-time down by 70%
- Defects down by 90%

What could that future organization accomplish? The organization could most likely develop new products and services in 50-75% less time at half the current development costs. It would also deliver products and services with significantly less production lead-time and at half the current production costs. This version of your organization does not exist today, but the achievement is not out of reach if the organization is motivated. Performance improvement like those listed above have been demonstrated at one or another Kazien Organizations. What is needed is the leadership to implement them all!

Process Kaizen

What are the Costs of Kaizen?

Very little capital investment is actually required. The main cost of implementing Kaizen is time. Time is required by the entire management team and workforce. Kaizen is not heavily reliant on technology within the enterprise and reduces the need for sophisticated, complex approaches to production management and information systems by first focusing on the people and process components of the organization.

Typical Costs of the Kaizen Journey

- Time – people
- Education and Training – people
- Tools Development – process & technology
- Management Information Systems Development - technology

How the Kaizen Journey Provides a Return on Investment (ROI)

Typically, the savings from reduced inventory levels alone are greater than all the costs of converting to Lean and Kaizen. In fact, your Kaizen Journey should actually reduce capital investment and other resources over the long run. Freed-up floor space becomes available for future expansion, or may be rented or sold. Shortened product development lead times also result in reduced resource requirements.

Understanding Lean Thinking

What is Lean Thinking?

Lean Thinking is delivering exactly what customers want, when they need it, in the quantity they need it, in the right sequence, without defects, and at the lowest possible cost.

Guiding Principles of Lean (See Index for more on each)	
• Identify and eliminate waste	• Achieve flow
• Specify and focus on value	• Build pull systems
• Map the value stream	• Pursue perfection

Lean Thinking	Traditional Thinking
• Small batches based on flow	• Batch and queue
• Production based on customer demand	• Production based on forecast
• Plant and equipment layout is based on product flow	• Plant and equipment layout is based on department function
• High worker empowerment	• Low worker empowerment
• Low inventory levels	• High inventory levels
• High flexibility	• Low flexibility
• Just in Time mentality	• Just in case mentality

Traditional Lean Tools Used in Obtaining Results (See Index for more on each)

- **6S (AKA 5S, 5S + 1)** - Organizes and standardizes the workplace
- **Visual Controls and Management** – Establishes signals to understand conditions or situations
- **Kanban** – Visual system for maintaining an orderly flow of material
- **Standardized Work** – Defines the best known waste-free processes and procedures
- **Value Stream Mapping** – Documents process relationships and exposes wastes
- **Total Productive Maintenance (TPM)** – Builds proactive and progressive operator maintenance
- **TAKT Time** – Sets production rate equal to customer demand rate
- **Work Cells** – Arranges operations and people in a cell (U-Shaped, etc.)
- **Pull Systems** – Produces parts and products based on customer demand
- **Quick Changeovers, Setup Reduction, and Single Minute Exchange of Dies** – Establishes the rapid changeover of equipment and reduced setup time
- **Error Proofing (AKA Poka Yoke)** – Prevents incorrect parts from being made or assembled; Identifies a flaw or error
- **Batch Size Reduction** – Reduces work in process (WIP) and improves lead times and cycle times
- **Concurrent Engineering** – Uses cross-functional teams to develop and bring products to market

What's the difference between Six Sigma, DMAIC, Lean and Kaizen?

Essentially, after we have streamlined our processes and activities using Lean thinking, we need to make sure that critical variables in the process perform consistently and repeatedly. Kaizen is a Japanese word meaning "good change" and is embodied by high impact events where incremental continuous improvement is implemented by cross-functional teams working together directly where the work gets done. Six Sigma is a tool based methodology that reduces variation in processes to increase customer satisfaction and improve the bottom line. To pursue perfection in processes, Six Sigma's Define, Measure, Analyze, Improve, Control (DMAIC) methodology identifies and isolates sources of variation and leverages a variety of tools to systematically reduce or eliminate the variation. Six Sigma helps organizations reduce waste in the form of variation and ultimately arrive at the best ways to deliver value to customers.

Understanding Six Sigma

Six Sigma is a structured methodology used to identify, quantify, eliminate and control sources of variation in processes. Six Sigma uses the define, measure, analyze, improve, and control (DMAIC) approach to problem solving.

Guiding Principles of Six Sigma	
• Process variability is proportional to costs and defects • Define the underlying problems • Measure where you are and where you want to be	• Leverage and analyze data in decision making • Improve the critical variables of the process • Control the process after you fix it to make sure you don't slip

Traditional Six Sigma Tools Used in Obtaining Results (See Index)
• **Process Capability** - A statistical measure of the inherent process variability of a given characteristic. The most widely accepted formula for process capability is six sigma.   • **Process Mapping** - A type of flowchart depicting the steps in a process and identifying responsibility for each step and key measures.   • **Data Collection** - A set of collected facts. There are two basic kinds of numerical data: measured or variable data, such as "16 ounces," "4 miles" and "0.75 inches;" and counted or attribute data, such as "162 defects."   • **Critical to Satisfaction Measures (CT Flowdown)** – The primary method for scoping project opportunities.   • **Cause and Effect Analysis** - A tool for analyzing process dispersion. It is also referred to as the "Ishikawa diagram," because Kaoru Ishikawa developed it, and the "fishbone diagram," because the complete diagram resembles a fish skeleton. The diagram illustrates the main causes and sub-causes leading to an effect (symptom). The

Traditional Six Sigma Tools Used in Obtaining Results (See Index)

cause and effect diagram is one of the "seven tools of quality."

- **5 Whys** - A technique for discovering the root causes of a problem and showing the relationship of causes by repeatedly asking the question, "Why?"
- **Failure Modes and Effects Analysis** - A systematized group of activities to recognize and evaluate the potential failure of a product or process and its effects, identify actions that could eliminate or reduce the occurrence of the potential failure and document the process.
- **Measurement Systems Analysis (MSA)** A method for evaluating how much variation occurs in the process by which we collect data.
- **Data Sampling** - One or more units of product (or a quantity of material) drawn from a lot for purposes of inspection to reach a decision regarding acceptance of the lot.
- **Hypothesis and Regression Testing** - A statistical technique for determining the best mathematical expression describing the functional relationship between one response and one or more independent variables.
- **Standard Operations**- A precise description of each work activity, specifying cycle time, takt time, the work sequence of specific tasks and the minimum inventory of parts on hand needed to conduct the activity. All jobs are organized around human motion to create an efficient sequence without waste. Work organized in such a way is called standard(ized) work.
- **Design on Experiment** - A branch of applied statistics dealing with planning, conducting, analyzing and interpreting controlled tests to evaluate the factors that control the value of a parameter or group of parameters.
- **Statistical Process Control (SPC)** - The application of statistical techniques to control a process
- **Control and Reaction Plans** - Written descriptions of the systems for controlling part and process quality by addressing the key characteristics and engineering requirements.
- **Control Charts** - A chart with upper and lower control limits on which values of some statistical measure for a series of samples or subgroups are plotted. The chart frequently shows a central line to help detect a trend of plotted values toward either control limit.

Understanding 6S (AKA 5S, 5S+1)

What is 6S?

6S is a simple starting point in Lean Thinking that helps organizations create and maintain an organized, clean, and high performance workplace for safer and effective operation.

Guiding Principles of 6S	
• Communicate the job to be done • Organize the work area and	• Reduce in-process defects and costs • Standardize work practices

equipment • Eliminate wasted time and motion	• Create a safer workplace

What are the 6S's?	Key Take Away
Sort	Eliminate unnecessary items from work area
Straighten	Arrange the workplace with necessary items
Shine	Establish the image of high quality capability
Standardize	Use standard methods to sort, straighten and shine
Sustain	Maintain the gains through empowerment, commitment, and discipline
Safety	Zero accidents and injuries!

What are the signs that a work area needs 6S?

- Space is crowded with parts and tools
- Equipment is dirty and the workplace unorganized
- Too many "things" are packed into storage spaces
- Work areas and surfaces are used as storage spaces instead of work spaces
- Information is posted and available, yet nobody knows what is going on
- Accidents are just waiting to happen
- Administrative work areas are unorganized or cluttered

What's the difference between 6S, 5S (5S+1), Visual Controls, and Total Productive Maintenance?

6S is an evolutionary process that has compiled best practices in organization and cleaning over the past 50 years. Originally this process was known as 5S, which was based on a method of organization and housekeeping at Toyota. It was known as 5S because it contained five activities that in the Japanese language all began with the letter "S" – Seiri, Seiton, Seiso, Seiketsu, Shitsuke. During the 1990's, as American companies began adopting the process, the activities were translated into corresponding English words that also began with the letter "S". In addition to adopting the methodology, American managers found it critical to include safety as an additional "S" and coined the term "5S+1" to add visibility to the safety element.

Visual Controls are simple signals often used in 6S to provide an immediate and readily apparent understanding of a condition or situation. 6S Visual Controls should be efficient, self-regulating, and worker managed and may include Kanban cards, lights, color coding, and lines for delineation of work areas or product flow.

Total Productive Maintenance, also referred to as TPM, becomes an evolutionary step in the 6S process as proactive and progressive maintenance methodologies emerge from the completion of initial activities and the adoption of standardized practices for Sorting,

Straightening, and Shining. TPM directly contributes to reductions in operating costs, longer equipment life, and lower overall maintenance costs for any organization.

Understanding Visual Controls and Management with Kanban

Visual Controls and Management is a system that enables any person to immediately recognize standards and information as well as any problems, abnormalities, waste or deviations from standards.

Guiding Principles of Visual Controls and Management	
• Extremely visible and easily understood • Detect and prevent abnormalities • Local ownership	• Build standards into the workplace • Communicate established standards • Share information and results

The Visual Control Pyramid

The visual Control Pyramid below shows that 6S is the foundation of Visual Management. After clutter, dirt and unnecessary items have been eliminated from the target area, many irregularities in process and flow become evident. Visual displays and controls can be leveraged to continuously improve control over the inputs going into the process.

"The Control Pyramid"

Types of Visual Controls	Visual Management Intent
• Pull Cards • Light Signal • Bins • Flags • Totes • Exchange Containers – Empty bins signals need • Empty spaces or shelves • Bar coded labels • Lines and arrows on floors • Minimum and maximum quantity indicators • Production Boards	**Ensure:** • The **right thing** • In the **right quantity** • At the **right time** • To the **right location** • In the **right orientation** **Create simple signs that can:** • Trigger material replenishment • Stop production • Communicate production goals

Visual Management

A Visual Management System is a <u>system</u> that enables any person (even those who know very little about a specific work area) to immediately recognize standards and information as well as any problems, abnormalities, waste or deviations from standards.

The Five Forms of Visual Control	
• Visual Standardized Work Methods • Visual Production/Process Control • Visual Quality Control	• Visual Process Indicators • Visual "5S"

Understanding Pull Systems and One Piece Flow

Pull Systems are the preferred Lean model because they operate on the least possible work in process and result in the shortest lead time. In contrast to the other systems, Pull Systems are a disciplined approach because the system won't allow material to be pushed through unless the next process needs it. Pull Systems may still use materials requirements planning for long lead time materials, but for the most part production is tied to actual demand. In Pull Systems, inventory and lead times are greatly reduced. By relying heavily on visual signals, Pull Systems quickly streamline the process, expose abnormalities, and improve quality of products and services.

Guiding Principles of Pull Systems	
• Treat inventory as a liability! • Strive to a batch size of one • Continuously reduce setup time • Eliminate non-value added activities	• Dramatically shorten cycle times • Standardize operations • Synchronize production processes • Practice visual management

The Toyota Production System is frequently modeled as a house with two pillars. One pillar represents just-in-time (JIT) and the other pillar represents the concept of Jidoka. The Jidoka pillar is often referred to as Autonomation. The concept has two elements – fool proof quality control and autonomous equipment operation. By modifying a process to operate without constant operator intervention frees the operator to perform other tasks, thus increasing productivity. However, for the operator to have confidence in walking away from the equipment, controls must be in place that will not allow the process to make/pass a bad product.

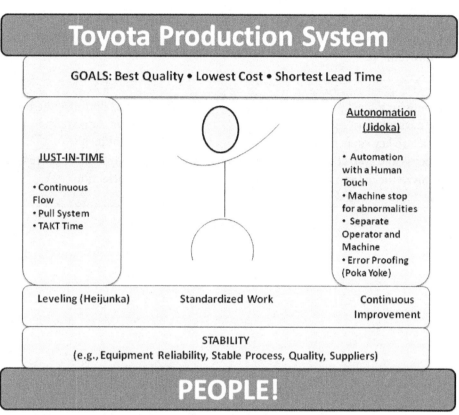

Example of Pull System	Benefits of Pull Systems
Production Smoothing (AKA Heijunka) • Keeps production volume as constant as possible • Enables consistent work flow • Takes into account both volume and mix • **GOAL: Produce any product any day!**	• Improves customer response • Maintains a consistent output of product • Minimizes work in process • Minimizes finished goods inventory • Reduces the requirements of capital investment • Reduces rework and scrap • Improves on time delivery

	• Reduces the impact of surprises

Understanding the DMAIC Methodology

What is DMAIC (Pronounced *Duh-May-Ick*)?

DMAIC is a best in class improvement model that uses a data driven strategy for improving processes and empowers teams with the roadmap and tools to succeed at sustainable process improvement.

Guiding Principles of DMAIC	
• Define high-level project goals and the current process • Measure key aspects of the current process and collect the relevant data • Analyze the data to verify cause and effect relationships	• Improve or optimize the process based upon data analysis and best in class techniques • Statistically control processes • Pursue perfection

DMAIC Cycle

Process Kaizen

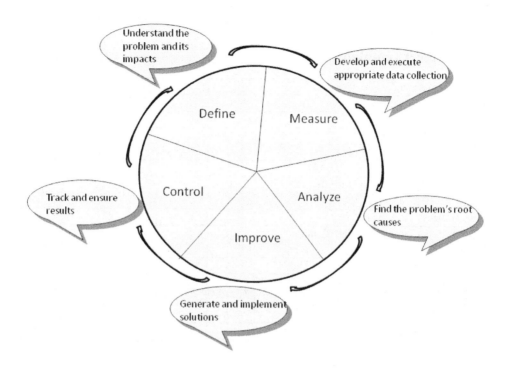

Understanding the DMAIC Acronym	Key Tools and Deliverables
Define	Problem/Opportunity Statement, Project Objective, Primary Output Metrics, Defect Definition, Stakeholder Analysis, Critical to Satisfaction Measures, High-level Process Map
Measure	Detailed Process Map, Value Stream Map, Baseline Process Capability, Measurement Systems Analysis, Project Data Collection Plan
Analyze	Cause and Effect Analysis, Failure Modes and Effects Analysis
Improve	Future State Process Map, Improvements and Operating Tolerances, Performance Statistics
Control	Hypothesis Testing, Control Plan, Reaction Plan, Standard Operating Procedures, Statistical Process Control

When should you use DMAIC?
- To find permanent solutions to long-standing or tricky business problems
- To identify causes and solutions that are not obvious due to complex process
- To mitigate solution risks when risks are high

- To methodically develop, test, and refine solution ideas before imposing them on workplace
- To use data logically to show the best solution

DMAIC Project Template

Define	Hours	
Kickoff	1	
Current State SIPOC (TEAM)	1	
Current State Process Map		
Level 1 Process Map (TEAM)	.5	
Level 2 Process Maps (TEAM)	2	
Process Inputs and Outputs (TEAM)	1	
Measure		Define Completed
Process Metrics		
Process Times and Wait Times (TEAM)	.5	
Value Added Flow Analysis (TEAM)	.5	
Process Metrics Summary (TEAM)	.5	
Analyze		Measure Completed
Cause and Effect Analysis (TEAM)	1.5	
Failure Modes and Effects Analysis (TEAM)	1.5	
Improve		Analyze Completed
Implement Improvements (TEAM)	24	
v1 Procedures (TEAM)	2	
Total Team Commitment in Hours	32	

DMAIC Project Deliverables

SIPOC
A tool used by process improvement teams to identify all relevant elements (suppliers, inputs, process, outputs, customers) before work begins.

Process Maps
A process is a set of interrelated work activities characterized by a set of specific inputs and value added tasks that make up a procedure for a set of specific outputs. Process Maps are a type of flowchart depicting the steps in a process and identifying responsibility for each step and key measures. Process design is iterative.

Process Inputs and Outs
Process inputs and outputs allow process team members to bring their personal, regional, and industry experience while documenting key variables that deliver value to the customer in the form of process outputs. By gathering perspectives from each team member, we can then analyze what inputs are influenced by regional variables and which inputs can be leveraged as best practices nationwide and across the enterprise. Process inputs and outputs are also required to continue the DMAIC process (Analyze Phase).

Process Metrics and Value Added Flow Analysis

Process Metrics are standard measures used to assess the performance of a particular operation or activity. The improvement team focuses on one to three high-level performance measures for each sub-process identified to help identify important outputs, customer requirements, and business needs for the process. Value Added Flow Analysis allows teams to work with a uniform definition of value to better recognize and eliminate waste while focusing on the real value that the process is delivering to the customer.

Cause and Effect Analysis

Cause and Effect Analysis is a qualitative approach that attempts to quantify the correlation of "How Important" certain inputs are relative to achieving "Goals" represented by certain outputs. Cause and Effect Analysis creates a prioritized list of inputs for further analysis.

Failure Modes and Effects Analysis

Failure Modes and Effects Analysis provides a structured approach to identifying the ways in which a product or process can fail, estimating the risk associated with specific causes, and prioritizing the actions that should be taken to reduce the risk. The primary directive during analysis is to identify ways the product or process can fail and eliminate or reduce the risk of failure in order to protect the customer.

The Kaizen Event Process

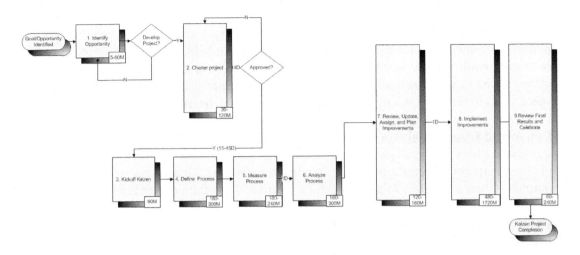

Overview

Kaizen Events are weeklong intensive process improvement projects where 5-8 subject matter experts are brought together to work on a scoped project charter and problem statement. The project team is expected to be available for 40 hours to participate in the event and implement improvements. Kaizen Events primarily focus on eliminating waste as well as streamlining and speeding up the process. The Kaizen Event process involves business stakeholders identifying and communicating opportunities for improvement to a Kaizen Facilitator. Kaizen Facilitators are trained to collect baseline performance data, charter Kaizen Event opportunities, kick off and manage projects and facilitate process definition, measurement, analysis, improvement and control, all within a rapid improvement project environment.

Objectives

- Incrementally improve processes
- Define the current state of processes
- Expose and eliminate waste
- Standardize and Visually Manage the process
- Identify and fix the root causes of key issues

Process Kaizen

1. Identify Opportunity

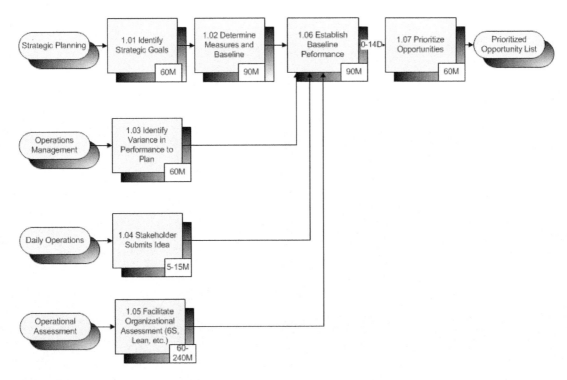

Overview

During the Identify Opportunity sub-process, a variety of process stakeholders, coordinated by the Kaizen Facilitator, identify and begin to scope opportunities for improvement in particular process areas. Methods for identifying opportunities include Strategic Planning, Operations Management, Daily Operations, and Operational Assessments. Kaizen Facilitators also assist in scoping and collecting data, establishing baseline performance capability, and prioritizing Kaizen Event opportunities for chartering.

Objectives

- Align improvement opportunities to strategic imperatives
- Take action on variances in performance to plan
- Listen to process stakeholders
- Assess the organization and process against best practices and standards

1.01 Identify Strategic Goals

Overview

During the Identify Strategic Goals activity, the Kaizen Facilitator gathers any existing documentation related to the organization's or department's strategic goals and objectives, validates existing documentation with stakeholders perceptions, and summarizes the critical goals and objectives that will influence opportunity identification and project selection. The Kaizen Facilitator may engage any number of process stakeholders at this stage to identify organization vision and strategic imperatives, department goals, stakeholder perceptions, and discovery around the current state and possible future states of the process.

Objective

- Understand the importance of vision and strategy on process intent and execution
- Align process improvement efforts to the strategic needs of the organization

Estimated Time to Complete

120 to 240 Minutes

Inputs (Resources required by the process)	Where/From
Kaizen Facilitator	You
Project Sponsors/ Process Owners	Organization
Stakeholders	Organization
Understanding Kaizen Opportunities	Figure 1.01.01
Strategic Goals	Organization
Strategic Objectives Discovery Template	Figure 1.01.02

Outputs (Deliverables from the process)	Possible Metrics
Understanding of Strategic Goals	Time to Review; Number of Questions; Key Performance Indicators

Steps to Complete

1. Lean Facilitator gathers and reviews any documented strategic goals or imperatives

2. Lean Facilitator develops strategy assessment and/or surveys

3. Analyze results of strategy assessments and/or survey

4. Summarize strategy assessments and surveys

5. Summarize top 5 Strategic Objectives

Figure 1.01.01 - Understanding Kaizen Opportunities

Understanding Kaizen Opportunities

We scope Kaizen opportunities by driving project ideas from general to specific. You can identify opportunities in a variety of ways and through a variety of methods. Creating a standard way of identifying and defining Kaizen opportunities is important because you will be applying valuable human resources to solving mission critical, and often time sensitive, business problems. Many organizations use three key focus areas, such as the approach below, as venues for identifying opportunities.

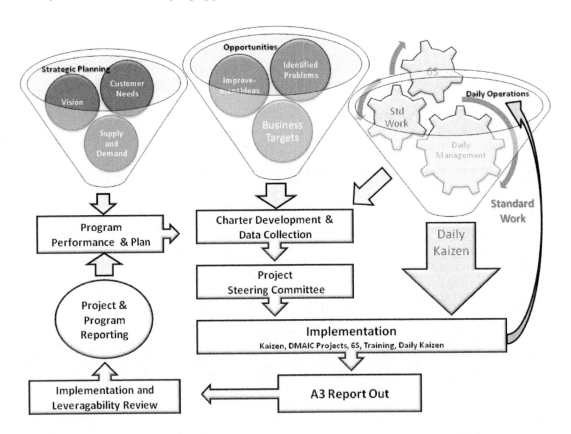

How do organizations use this model?

First, various areas of interest are identified through strategic planning (Vision, Process Intent and Operations 1-5 year plan), operational management, and daily operations standard work. Leadership teams then typically derive the factors that influence those areas of interest and then categorize and arrange the various business relationships and goals. Baseline data and costs can then be populated and attributed to the areas of influence and the leadership team can prioritize and select the critical components with the largest opportunity.

How can you arrive at key areas of interest for your organization?

By applying the 5 Critical Pathways to Identifying Opportunities

Identification Path	High Level Steps to Complete
Strategic Imperatives	1. Identify strategic goals 2. Drive to an actionable level 3. Establish current performance to the goal 4. Identify gaps between goals and current performance 5. Determine measures (metrics) of performance 6. Determine the factors that impact the goal
Performance to Plan	1. Historical budget performance to plan is analyzed 2. Identify ongoing performance gaps 3. Areas showing large gaps in performance are opportunities to identify project ideas • Use CT Flow Down to scope projects 4. When executing this pathway, to prevent chasing false opportunities, we need to understand whether the budgeted targets are realistic compared to benchmarks, best practice, etc.

Financial Analysis	1. The financial data of the Company is analyzed to determine whether financial measures are in line with industry, for example:
	   a. Inventory turns
	   b. Worker Compensation
	   c. Accounts Payable
	   d. Accounts Receivable
	   e. Productivity
	2. Gaps in these areas are potential opportunities for project ideas
	   • Use CT Flow Down to scope projects

Identification Path	High Level Steps to Complete

Organic Bubble-Up	1. Organic project definition
	
	   a. A project that may **not be strategic** in nature, but is a **good idea** and will save money or improve customer/employee satisfaction
	
	   b. **Brainstorming** and soliciting people's ideas and issues/**pain points**
	
	   c. Use CT Flow Down to scope the project ideas
	
	Examples of organic projects
	
	• Overpayment of taxes to U.S. Government
	• Poor measurement system for general merchandise inventory in drug stores
	• Excess cost in copiers, printers, fax machines
	
	Note: This pathway by itself is the least desirable method

Operational Assessment	1. Financial and product data are analyzed to determine where the greatest opportunity exists 2. Financial and product data are analyzed to segment the top 3-5 products/processes that afford the greatest opportunity 3. Facilitate the appropriate audit or assessment for the work area/product/service/process (6S Audit, Lean Organizational Audit, etc.)

What makes a good Kaizen Event opportunity?

Project Selection Criteria Checklist	Yes	No
1. Has the project been done already (or in progress)?		☑
2. Is there a pre-determined solution to the project goals?		☑
3. Does this project conflict with other projects?		☑
4. Does this project have a high probability of success?	☑	
5. Is the project linked/aligned to the goals of the business?	☑	
6. Does the cost reduction opportunity meet the goals of the business?	☑	
7. Has the project been properly scoped?	☑	
8. Can starting and end points for the process be defined?	☑	
9. Does the sponsor have functional control of the impacted process?	☑	
10. Are metrics available or could they be developed quickly at low cost?	☑	

Project Selection Criteria Checklist	Yes	No
11. Is data collection relatively easy?	☑	
12. Is there a "good" measurement system in place?	☑	
13. Are resources available and supportive of the project?	☑	
14. Can you define the defect in the process?	☑	

Figure 1.01.02 - Strategic Objectives Discovery Template

Overview Questions

1. What are your team/department/organization objectives?
2. What is your goal?
3. What's happening now?
4. If you could get anything at all out of process improvements, what would it be?
5. How is improvement important to you?

Current Process Questions

1. What is your evaluation of the current process as it relates to your department?
   a. What does the current process do well?
   b. What does the current process do not so well?
   c. What would you like to see different?
2. What is your evaluation of your department as it relates to the current process?
   a. What do you do well?
   b. What do you do not so well?
   c. What would you like to see different?
3. How well do you understand the current process?
4. How well do you understand and meet the demands of the current process?
5. Are there any issues or opportunities you would like to see addressed in the current process?

Future Process Questions

1. How could we make the process best for you?
2. What is your dream state?
3. How do you envision the relationship between your processes and other processes?

Education/Information

1. What are your current educational needs as they relate to the process?
2. Do you see those educational needs changing when we move to a new process? How?
3. What would you like us to focus on during the process improvement?

Technology

1. What technology interfaces are currently used?
2. Are there any issues or opportunities you would like to see addressed?
3. Do you have a vision of the technology you will need?

Training for Staff

1. What are your current training needs for staff as they relate to the current process?
2. Do you see those training needs changing when we move to a new process? How?
3. What would you like us to focus on during the new process training?

Discovery Session Summaries:

Requirements Gathering Translator

Use the following requirements gathering format to identify needs.

As a <Role> I need <functionality> so that I can <goal>.

Problems

Provide a narrative summary of the problems and issues identified with the current state process.

Expectations

Provide a narrative summary of the expectations identified with the future state of the process and improvements.

Discovery Areas

Identify core processes areas uncovered during the discovery session.

Discovery Checklist

1. Can the process be defined?
2. What is the estimate for completing process definition?
3. Does a problem in the process occur frequently enough to have been brought up during discovery?

4. Is the problem area well known and is there visibility within the organization or functional area?

5. Does improvement of this process seem important to leadership?
6. Will people appreciate if this process is improved?
7. Is there a good chance of success to improve this process?
8. Is there any current work being done to monitor, control, or improve this process?

9. Can potential changes to the process be completed with little to no outside help?
10. Are solutions being imposed on this process?

Discovery Objectives (Create the Beginnings of your Project Charter)

1. Process Description
2. Problem Statement
3. Primary Metric
4. Defect Definition
5. Assumptions, Risks and Obstacles

1.02 Determine Measure(s) and Baseline

Overview

During the Determine Measure(s) and Baseline activity, the Kaizen Facilitator identifies 1-3 primary output metrics for the process, identifies possible data sources, develops a plan, and extracts the baseline data. Baseline data can be anywhere from one week to two plus years of historical data.

Objective

- Understand the importance of data to Kaizen Events and process improvement
- Identify and analyze data sources
- Extract the necessary information to establish baseline performance

Estimated Time to Complete

120 to 480 Minutes

Inputs (Resources required by the process)	Where/From
Kaizen Facilitator	You
Project Sponsor; Process Owner	Organization
Understanding Primary Metrics Document	Figure 1.02.01
Collecting Baseline Data Document	Figure 1.02.02
Data Collection Plan	Figure 1.02.02

Outputs (Deliverables from the process)	Possible Metrics
Understanding of Process Primary Metric(s)	Time to Review; Number of Questions; Number of Parking Lot items

Outputs (Deliverables from the process)	Possible Metrics
Baseline Data	Time Period; Time to Collect Data; Primary Metric Average; Primary Metric Standard Deviation

Steps to Complete

1. Review Understanding of Primary Metrics and Collecting Baseline Data documents.

2. Identify 1-3 Primary Output Metrics

3. Identify and analyze possible data sources for data collection purposes

4. If necessary, negotiate access to key data sources with business partners and data stewards

5. Identify data elements within data sources and document reporting approaches

6. Extract data from data sources

7. Establish ongoing data delivery following the completion of Kaizen Event

Figure 1.02.01 – Understanding Primary Metrics

What are Primary Metrics?

Metrics are used to help define and measure the performance of a process. Different output measures are used to explain various aspects of performance and the most important process output measurements become the primary metrics of the process.

Why are Primary Metrics Important?

- Measure and track the output metrics of the process, including averages and standard deviation
- Represent the population of factors within the process ($Y=F(x^n)$)
- Provide views of trends or patterns in the process
- Allow for subsequent graphical interpretation, analysis and process improvement

The Principles Of Effective Organizational Measurement	
<ul><li>Fewer measures are better – Concentrate on the vital few</li><li>Link measures to key success factors</li><li>Use a mix of past, present, and</li></ul>	<ul><li>Base measures on expectations of customers and stakeholders</li><li>Use indices to give a better overall assessment of performance</li><li>Change measures as situation</li></ul>

The Principles Of Effective Organizational Measurement	
future measures	changes

What is baselining?

A baseline measurement is a beginning point, based on an evaluation of output over a period of time, used to determine the process parameters prior to any improvement effort and is the basis against which change is measured.

What is benchmarking?

Process benchmarking is a technique in which an organization measures its performance against that of best in class organizations or high performing internal groups, determines how those groups achieved their performance levels and uses the information to improve its own performance. Subjects that can be benchmarked include strategies, operations and processes. Benchmarking is a process used to achieve and sustain superior performance by learning from the best performers in the process and focusing on a creative integration of analysis and improvements to continuously improve performance. Benchmarking provides rigor, accountability, and is a great way to convince others that "we can do better." Benchmarking does require planning, analysis, commitment, improvement and follow-up in order to be successful.

What is Process Capability?

Process capability is a measurement of the capability of a process to deliver product or services that meet the needs of the customer as defined by the product/service specifications. It tells us how well the process is performing relative to customer expectations. Ultimately, the process should perform within the specifications of the customer.

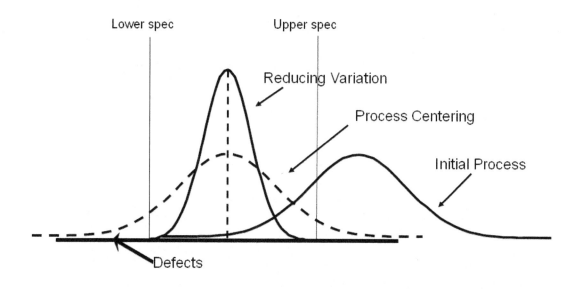

Figure 1.02.02 - Collecting Baseline Data

Understanding and Collecting Baseline Data

Data is used to help define the performance of your process. Different measures can be used to explain various aspects about performance and collecting baseline data is the first step to measuring the things that matter and driving improvements with metrics and measurements.

Two types of data: Continuous and Discrete

Continuous Data	Discrete Data
1. Information that can be measured on a continuum or scale is called "continuous data."	1. Information that is traditionally counted in whole numbers is known as "discrete data."
2. These measurements can typically be subdivided into smaller and smaller increments, depending on the precision of the measurement system.	2. You typically won't be able to immediately establish averages and standard deviations with discrete data. Instead, you will have to transform the data in some way so that it can be analyzed and summarized, so often it is best to try to convert the measurement to continuous data, which is more effective.
3. The power with using continuous data is that the mean, or average and standard deviation is easily used for performance analysis.	
4. Precision is the aspect of measurement that addresses repeatability or consistency when an identical item is	3. For example, instead of determining freshness of an item based on

Continuous Data	Discrete Data
measured several times. 5. Examples of continuous data include cost, length, time, weight, and temperature.	appearance we could count the number of days before or after the expiration data to judge how fresh it is. 4. Examples of discrete data include **count**, true or false, yes or no, and most other **classification** information like product type, brand, size, etc.

What is Data Collection?

For Kaizen, data collection is a process that provides the useful data necessary for subsequent graphical interpretation, analysis, and process improvement. Historically we have relied on our own belief systems and past experiences to determine what to measure and what to improve. Kaizen requires us to think about processes and using data to support changes and improvements to those processes. Data collection is the tool that provides the valid and useful information that will be analyzed to identify sources of variation and waste, to quantify their magnitude, and later to prove and monitor improvements. Without data, there is no analysis. Without data, decisions are made by "gut feel." Most importantly, without data there is NO proof of success.

Why is Data Collection Important?

Data Collection is important because it:	
• Empowers data driven decision making • Breaks down old paradigms and the status quo • Represents the population	• Represents the true current state of the process • Provides a view of trends or patterns in a process • Identifies data types and limitations in data collection and mathematical applicability

The Elements of a Data Collection Plan

Data Collection Plan Elements	
What to Measure	Utilize information gathered from "Customer Defined Measures" to: • Identify needs of the customer • How to measure those needs • Approach for collecting the appropriate data for each measure How do you find out what the customer cares about? Ask them!

Type of Measure	• What is the unit of output?
	
	• What makes it good or bad?
	
	• Describe the defect of interest
	
	    • <u>Sales Associate error</u>
	        - Incorrect Product Code entered
	        - Duplicate scan on one product purchased
	    • <u>Computer scanning error</u>
	        - Incorrect price
	    • <u>Inventory error</u>
	        - Product overstock
	        - Product out of stock

	Data Collection Plan Elements
Type of Data	1. Continuous – any measurement information 2. Discrete – Count – any counted information 3. Discrete – Classification – any categorized information
Operational Definition	<u>Operational Definition</u> is a clear, concise description of a measurement that provides a consistent understanding of: - What and how to measure
Data Collection Criteria	• Who will collect the data? • Has the definition of a defect or defective unit been well explained? • What issues or barriers could we run into? • What are the various cycles of the process? • Over what period of time will the data be collected?

Sampling Methods	Sampling is a procedure for selecting units to estimate a characteristic of the population; sample units should be representative of the population.
	
	Types of sampling:
	• Census
	• Convenience
	• Statistical
	    - Simple random sampling
	    - Stratified sampling
	    - Cluster sampling

Sampling Examples

Sampling is used to select a subset of the population of data to estimate or infer characteristics of the population. This is used when you can't deep dive every instance of data in the population.

Simple Random Sampling 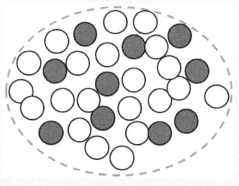	• Each "unit" has an equal chance of being selected • Simple • Unit = individual measure • Sub-group like units Example Scenario: To estimate the average height of the class, select 10 students at random. Calculate the average height of the sample.
Stratified Sampling 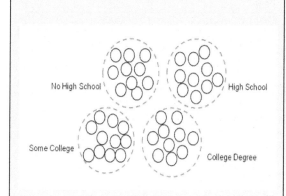	• Researchers may elect to evaluate <u>mutually exclusive strata</u> 　• Selecting individual units 　• Separate data by some factor (location, shift, product...) • Stratified random sampling: Random selection of individual units <u>within</u> strata • Useful when strata are expected to yield different results • Strata are suspected sources of variation • Unit = individual observation from each strata

1.03 Identify Variance in Performance to Plan

Overview

During the Identify Variance in Performance to Plan activity, a Process Owner identifies some discrepancy in performance to plan and does not immediately understand the root causes of the discrepancy. The Process Owner contacts the Kaizen Facilitator and helps to establish baseline performance. Identification of variation between performance and plan is generally established through strategic imperatives and operations goals.

Objective

- Understand current expectations and discrepancies in performance
- Communicate primary metrics and problem/opportunity statements to stakeholders
- Engage Kaizen Facilitator to validate performance data and assess opportunities

Estimated Time to Complete

5 to 60 Minutes

Inputs (Resources required by the process)	Where/From
Kaizen Facilitator	You
Process Owner	Organization
Operations Performance Metrics	Process Owner
Operations Performance Goals	Process Owner

Outputs (Deliverables from the process)	Possible Metrics
Performance to Plan Variance – Outside of Operating Tolerances	Percent Discrepancy
Problem/Opportunity Statement	Number of Opportunities

Steps to Complete

1. Review current period operations performance metrics

2. Identify "misses" in operational goals

3. Explore possible root causes for miss

3. Communicate the problem/opportunity to Kaizen Facilitator

Process Kaizen

1.04 Stakeholder Submits Idea

Overview

During the Stakeholder Submits Idea activity, various process stakeholders identify brief, easily communicated ideas and share them with the Kaizen Facilitator. The Kaizen Facilitator then screens the ideas to determine whether the opportunity should be researched or rejected. If a submitted idea should be researched, the Kaizen Facilitator attempts to establish the primary metrics for the idea and collects baseline performance data to scope the opportunity.

Objective

- Empower stakeholders to submit ideas for incremental process improvement
- Screen stakeholder ideas
- Identify primary metrics for process improvement ideas

Estimated Time to Complete

5 to 60 Minutes

Inputs (Resources required by the process)	Where/From
Kaizen Facilitator	You
Process Stakeholder	Internal and External Stakeholders
Making Ideas Visible Document	Figure 1.04.01
Idea	Stakeholder

Outputs (Deliverables from the process)	Possible Metrics
"Approved" Idea	Number of Submitted Ideas; Number of Approved Ideas
"Deferred" Idea	Number of Deferred Ideas

Steps to Complete

1. Stakeholder submits ideas to Kaizen Facilitator

2. Kaizen Facilitator screens ideas

3. Kaizen Facilitator researches opportunity and primary metrics

4. Kaizen Facilitator prioritizes opportunities for baseline performance data collection and project chartering

Figure 1.04.01 Making Ideas Visible

Making Ideas Visible

Ideas and stakeholder suggestion systems should be kept as straight forward as possible. The value add in managing and taking action on stakeholder ideas is NOT in assessing costs, prioritizing ideas, and recording information. The value add is to produce a steady stream of stakeholder-generated suggestions for improvement. In order for this to work, you need to believe in your stakeholders, whether they be your employees or your customers. You need to believe that they actually have ideas to contribute.

In a takt-paced Lean environment, no time is really available during the day for stakeholders to work on improvement activities outside of structured improvement events such as Kaizen Events. Most of peoples days are consumed with actual work – and there is no benefit to suggestions if nobody can work them. The benefit comes from implemented improvements. You first need to make these ideas visible and then commit the management resources to get the improvements done. The best, least waste way, with the least amount of overhead and cost is the Daily Kaizen Idea Board.

What is the Daily Kaizen Idea Board?

There is great power in making the improvement idea process visual. Posting suggestions for everybody to see provides an easily understood system that can encourage more ideas while visually controlling the suggestion process so people can see what has been submitted, what has been assigned, what is in progress and what is completed. Many organizations fail to listen to their stakeholders, employees, and customers. The Daily Kaizen Idea Board provides your stakeholders a vital opportunity to be heard and to see their ideas driven to completion.

Daily Kaizen Idea Board Example

Daily Kaizen Ideas Board

The Daily Kaizen Ideas Board is designed for employees to easily provide ideas that help make the process more effective and efficient and everyone's lives easier. The process is simple:

1. Write your idea on an "idea note"
2. Your site's Value Stream Manager will review and assign ideas on a daily basis
3. The assigned improvement point of contact will work on completing the idea
4. All lives are made easier when the idea is "done"

Idea	To Do	Doing	Done

Other Methods of Gathering Stakeholder Ideas	
Employee Suggestion Box	Employee Surveys
Customer Surveys	Human Sigma Surveys

Figure 1.04.02 Identifying Opportunities through an Andon Cord System

Understanding Andon Cords

What is an Andon Cord?

An Andon (Japanese word for "Lantern" or "Lamp") Cord is any visual and/or auditory signal that allows anyone in a work area to understand, at a glance, the current status of the process within the work area. Andon Cords are primarily used to signal that a defect has been identified in the process or that a stakeholder within the process needs help. We bring attention to quality or process issues as they occur through the use of Andon Cords.

Where does Andon Cord come from?

The original Andon Cord was a part of the manufacturing production line at Toyota. Along the assembly line, a rope – or "cord" – is strung up from beginning to end. This cord is accessible by every employee who is working on that particular production line.

How is it used?

As an employee works on the assembly line, they continually inspect every product as it passes through their station. If a problem – or defect – is detected, the employee would pull the "andon cord" to alert the team of the situation. Once the cord is activated, the production line halts, and the situation is immediately investigated and researched. Only when the issue is resolved is the line restarted and production resumed. The situation is then documented and further researched so similar issues can be prevented in the future.

Why is this important?

First and foremost, Andon Cord serves as a tool used to identify process defects so that they can be remedied before they cause issues further downstream in the process. Secondly, by documenting Andon Cord pulls, Management can continually study and learn from each defect as opportunity to improve the process to minimize the possibility of future defects. Finally, by encouraging front line workers to continually inspect the process, Andon Cord promotes responsibility and a sense of ownership for individual workers and promotes the belief that workers and all stakeholders in the process have ideas to improve the process.

The Guiding Principles of Andon Cords

1. Make it VERY clear when help is needed (Must be visual and/or audio)

2. Make the status of the process clear to EVERYBODY (At a glance)

3. Empower everyone to identify abnormal conditions in the process (Everyone pulls Andon Cords every day)

The Guiding Principles of Andon Cords (continued)

4. Train everyone to trace back issues and eliminate root causes (Failure Modes Effects and 5Y Analysis)

5. Support Andon Cords by monitoring the work area and responding to Andon Cords (within agreed upon time)

Why use Andon Cords?

- An easy and inexpensive system for identifying problems and deviations
- The status of the process is easily understood at a glance
- Stakeholders understand the value they are contributing to the organization
- Easiest method for real-time issues escalation, troubleshooting, and resolution

4 Steps to Implementing Andon Cords

1. Identify the work area and the process (Identify Activities and Metrics)

2. Select the media to be used for the Andon Cord (Must be Visual)

3. Establish the Andon Cord Trigger and Response Process (Who needs an Andon Cord? Who responds? How fast?)

4. Engage the work force to identify and eliminate waste (Standard Work for Andon Cord Process; Track Improvement)

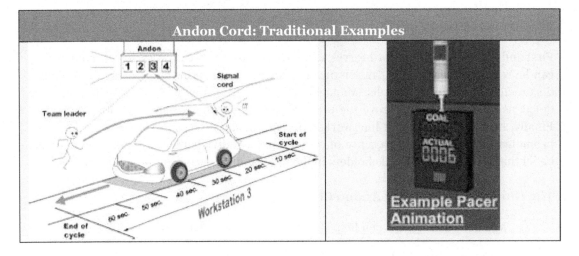

When combined with the Ideas Board, Shift Start Up Meetings, and other Daily Kaizen tools, Andon Cords can be a powerful tool to help management create a positive environment where front line resolvers can feel supported and customers feel appreciated.

How to succeed at implementing Andon Cords

There is more to Andon Cords (of course) than just triggering a visual or auditory signal. You need to have the processes in place and the resource available to respond to those Andon Cords. In fact, monitoring the work area for Andon Cords is one of the most important activities a management team can perform. By quickly responding to Andon Cords as they are pulled on the production floor, Leads and Managers are closer to the process and the customer and are able to research and troubleshoot with associates in real-time as the associates encounter defects in the process. The most important ways a management team can support Andon Cords are:

1. Schedule resources for adequate coverage of the work area to primarily respond to Andon Cords

2. Respond to Andon Cords quickly, within established response times or service levels agreements

3. Track Andon Cord reasons and identify opportunities for process improvement

4. Observe and listen to the process – trigger a "Lead Andon Cord" when non-standard work is identified or an over-the-shoulder coaching opportunity is identified

5. Reinforce submission of ideas to the ideas board

6. Build daily accountability and discipline in Daily Kaizen activities – Shift Startup, Andon Cords, Visual Management

1.05 Facilitate Organizational Assessment

Overview

During the Facilitate Organizational Assessment activity, the Kaizen Facilitator can apply a variety of Organizational Assessments in order to establish a baseline performance capability related to Lean, Process Capability, 6S, or other measurement criteria. These Assessments may be applied in a variety of work areas within the organization as well as generally applied to the entire organization. The results of the Organizational Assessments assist the Kaizen Facilitator in establishing baseline performance for critical areas of the organization. Based on the results of each assessment, the Kaizen Facilitator may identify and collect baseline performance data in order to better scope the opportunity.

Objective

- Understand the different Organizational Assessments available
- Establish the benchmark for the Organizational Assessment
- Facilitate Organizational Assessment and identify improvement opportunities

Estimated Time to Complete

5 to 240 Minutes

Inputs (Resources required by the process)	Where/From
Kaizen Facilitator	You
Project Sponsor; Process Owner	Organization
Process Stakeholders	Internal and External Stakeholders
Organizational Assessment(s)	Figures 1.05.01 and 1.05.02

Outputs (Deliverables from the process)	Possible Metrics
Organizational Assessment Results	Time to Review; Number of Questions; Number of Parking Lot items

Steps to Complete

1. Review available Organizational Assessments

2. Complete selected Organization Assessment(s)

3. Calculate and analyze Assessment results

4. Identify targeted areas for opportunity and identify primary metrics and measures

5. Collect data (manually if necessary) to establish current performance for targeted area

Figure 1.05.01 – Lean Organization Assessment Example

Important Steps in Lean Transformation	Key Questions on Lean Practice	Score (0,1,4, or 9)	Reasons for Lean Practice
Enterprise Strategic Planning	Does Lean appear integrated into planning?		Create an impact to value based on cycle time and capability
	Is there an obvious focus on customer value?		Customers pull value from the value stream
	Are teams leveraging the extended enterprise for the customer?		Value stream extends from customer throughout the organization
Lean Paradigm	Is there learning and education in Lean for associates?		Capable of "unlearning" the old and learning the new
	Are managers committed to Lean?		Management personally leading
	Is the Lean vision clearly communicated to associates?		Associates have a new mental model of the enterprise
	Do associates share a sense of urgency about Lean?		Sense of urgency is the primary driving force behind lean
Focus on the Value Stream	Do associates understand the value stream?		We must know how we deliver value to customers
	Do associates understand the concept of flow?		Single piece flow of materials and information is the most efficient flow
	Do associates design future value streams?		Value stream must meet the enterprise vision
	Do associates track performance		Performance measure drive enterprise behaviors

Process Kaizen

Important Steps in Lean Transformation	Key Questions on Lean Practice	Score	Reasons for Lean Practice
	measures?		
Lean Structure and Behavior	Is Lean organization orientation present?		Enterprise must be organized to support value delivery
	Are relationships based on mutual trust?		Win-Win vs. Us-Them
	Is there open and timely communication?		Open information exchange when required
	Is associate empowerment evident?		Decision should be made at the lowest possible level
	Are incentives designed around lean behaviors?		We must reward the behavior we want
	Is innovation encouraged?		Organization should be focused on risk rewarding instead of risk aversion
	Are there Lean change agents present?		Every organization must have inspiration and drivers of change
Create/Refine a Plan	Is there an organizational Lean transformation plan available?		Chart the course across the extended enterprise
	Are resources committed to Lean improvements?		Resources must be provided for lean transformation
	Is education and training provided on Lean?		Just-in-time learning should be the standard
Lean Initiatives	Are detailed plans developed based on the organization's plans?		Lean improvements must be coordinated
	Is tracking		Lean program must assess

Important Steps in Lean Transformation	Key Questions on Lean Practice	Score	Reasons for Lean Practice
	implemented for reporting improvement results?		actual outcomes against goals
Focus on Continuous Improvement	Are process improvement processes structured?		There must be uniformity in how we get better
	Is Lean progress monitored?		We must assess progress toward achieving organization objectives
	Is the Lean process nurtured?		Senior Leaders must be involved in the Lean transformation
	Are lessons learned captured?		Ensure that successes lead to more successes
	Is Lean impacting enterprise strategic planning?		Ensure that Lean results lead to strategic opportunities
Transform the Enterprise	Is Lean capability leveraged for new opportunities?		Organization should exploit new opportunities arising from lean enabled capabilities
	Are capability and utilization of assets optimized using Lean?		Lean enables mission growth through the redeployment of assets
	Is Lean leveraged to manage risk, cost, schedule, and performance?		Success follows effective risk management
	Are resources allocated for lean project development efforts?		The entire organization should team for success
Build Relationships	Are relationships with stakeholders defined and developed?		Aligning stakeholder values through relationships that build credibility

Process Kaizen

Important Steps in Lean Transformation	Key Questions on Lean Practice	Score	Reasons for Lean Practice
	Are relationships among stakeholders effective?		Create effective relationships to achieve customer value
	Is innovation and knowledge-sharing fostered between stakeholders		Incentivizing innovation through stakeholder involvement
Develop the Plan	Have requirements be defined around value and the lifecycle of the process?		Stakeholder pull vs. technology/product push
	Is data captured from the extended enterprise to optimize future requirements?		Closed loop processes capture operational performance data
	Is stakeholder value incorporated into the design of services and processes?		Understanding stakeholder value facilitates fewer development disturbances
	Is there a multidisciplinary approach to improvement?		Breakdown functional silos and enable seamless communication and value flow
Implement the Plan	Is Lean used in decision making?		Stakeholder capability should be strategically leveraged
	Is Lean fostered throughout the value stream?		Stakeholder innovation and flexibility should be promoted
	Are customer requirements and expectations with the extended organization?		Customer and stakeholder expectations should be aligned
	Are services transitioned to production in a lean fashion?		Always have the right product for a ready customer

Important Steps in Lean Transformation	Key Questions on Lean Practice	Score	Reasons for Lean Practice
Learn, Improve, and Sustain	Does the organization enhance the value of delivered services to the customer?		Respond to the voice of the customer
	Are post delivery service, support and sustainability provided?		Provide customer solutions
Lean System Enablers	Financial benefits translation of primary process metrics?		Lean requires the appropriate financial data
	Stakeholders have access to pull information?		Data should be available on demand
	Is the Learning Organization model in place?		Learning organizations create a flexible workforce
	Is the Lean enterprise enabled by information systems and tools?		Lean organizations facilitate the flow of information and knowledge
	Is environmental protection, health, and safety present in the system?		Lean organizations are cleaner, healthier, and safer
Lean Process Enablers	Are processes sustained with standard work?		Strive for consistency and reuse
	Are there common tools and systems?		Assure compatibility, reduce costs
	Is there a focus on variation reduction?		Reduce uncertainty by reducing variation

Figure 1.05.02 – 6S Audit Examples

How to Complete 6S Audit of Target Area

Overview

The 6S Audit is a tool that can help you understand the 6S issues in a target area. You can use the 6S Audit Form to quickly assess and organize the 6S categories of Sort, Straighten, Shine, Standardize, Sustain and Safety broken down into line items based on targeted conditions. By rating the target area in this way you will learn a great deal about 6S and have a baseline of performance measurement for the targeted area.

Objectives

- Perform an assessment of the target area's current conditions
- Score the results of the 6S Audit
- Determine a future date for a second assessment
- Identify areas of improvement

Time to Complete

30 to 60 Minutes

Inputs	Where/From
6S Audit Form	Figure 1.05.03
6S Participant(s)	You
Target Area	Shop, Job Site or Office
6S Audit Procedure	Figure 1.05.02
6S Audit Scoring Guidelines	Figure 1.05.03

Outputs	Possible Metrics
Completed 6S Audit Form	Audit Score
Areas of Improvement Notes	Number of Areas of Improvement Notes

Steps to Complete

1. Choose 6S participants responsible for the 6S Audit
2. Print the 6S Audit Form
3. Enter the date of the 6S Audit
4. For the entire target area, enter the score in the box next to each line item
5. Determine how many problems exist for each line item
6. Enter the 6S score based on the 6S Audit Scoring Guidelines for each line item
7. After rating each line item, add all the lines for each 6S category
8. After rating each 6S category, add all the lines and enter the total 6S Audit score
9. Document Areas of Improvement based on score lower than 3

Process Kaizen

Figure 1.05.03 – 6S Audit Form

6S Audit Form				
Auditor(s) _____ Work Area _____	**Scoring Key** Very good (0 problems or not applicable) = 4 Points Good (1-2 problems) = 3 Points Okay (3-4 problems) = 2 Points Poor (5-6 problems) = 1 Point Very Poor (7 or more problems) = 0 Points			
Category	**Issues**	Date ___	Date ___	Date ___
Sort	Non-essential or unorganized materials			
	Non-essential paperwork			
	Broken or non-essential equipment			
	Non-essential Tools			
	Obsolete or non-essential furniture			
Straighten	Items in clearly marked and effective positions			
	Containers boxes and bins organized and labeled			
	Maximum and minimum quantities indicated			
	Paperwork transactions arranged for easy pick up and return			
	Work area, tools, and equipment are numbered, named, color coded, etc.			
	All equipment locations defined			
Shine	Containers, boxes, and bins are clean			
	Tools are clean and in good working order			
	Ground is free of debris; Floors are free of dirt and debris			

6S Audit Form

	Stored cleaning equipment is available			
	Work area is organized to maintain cleanliness			
Standardize	6S Standards are known and visible			
	Roles and responsibilities are assigned and posted to maintain the first 3 Ss			
	6S Poster and/or Checklist posted			
	All necessary information posted			
	Ventilation and lighting is adequate			
Sustain	Cleaning activities are habitual and done voluntarily			
	Command media and job aides are up to date and effective			
	A system is in place to remind workers of the standards			
	Established standards are followed			
	The team takes initiative to do 6S			
Safety	Work areas requiring Personal Protective Equipment are clearly label			
	Fire hoses and emergency equipment are prominently displayed and unobstructed			
	Tripping dangers such as cables are removed from walking/standing areas			
	Emergency exits are available and easy			
	Walkways are unobstructed			
	Overall Total:			

6S Audit Scoring Guidelines

Scoring Key
Very good (0 problems or not applicable) = 4 Points
Good (1-2 problems) = 3 Points
Okay (3-4 problems) = 2 Points
Poor (5-6 problems) = 1 Point
Very Poor (7 or more problems) = 0 Points

1.06 Establish Baseline Performance

Overview

During the Establish Baseline Performance activity, the Kaizen Facilitator reviews the baseline performance data for the goals and metrics selected. The Kaizen Facilitator establishes the average performance for the period of measurement and calculates the standard deviation for the processes performance. The Kaizen Facilitator then summarizes the current gaps between the established goal and the historical performance of the process. The results of this initial performance to goal analysis will begin to scope the opportunity for the Kaizen Event.

Objective

- Understand the current performance of the process
- Understand the gaps between current process performance and the established goal

Estimated Time to Complete

60 to 480 Minutes

Inputs (Resources required by the process)	Where/From
Kaizen Facilitator	You
Baseline Data	Data Sources
Understanding Baseline Performance Reports	Figure 1.06.01
Analysis Tools	Organization

Outputs (Deliverables from the process)	Possible Metrics
Baseline Performance Report	Performance Average, Performance Variation, Percentage from Goal,

Steps to Complete

1. Review the gathered historical data (4-104 weeks of continuous data)

2. Review the Understanding Baseline Performance Reports document.

3. Establish the average and standard deviation for the performance measurement

4. Calculate performance averages and standard deviation for baseline historical data

5. Compare historical performance averages with established goals

6. Identify gaps and areas for performance improvement

Figure 1.06.01 Understanding Baseline Performance Reports

What is a Baseline Performance Report?

A Baseline Performance Report is the culmination of a process capability study that defines customer requirements in the form of operational definitions and operating tolerances, data collection that allows for analysis of short and long-term variation.

What questions do Baseline Performance Reports answer?	
• How is the process currently performing? • How well could the process perform?	• What can be expected tomorrow, next week, next month, and over the year? • Are customers' expectations being met?

Components of a Baseline Performance Report	
Process Performance	**S Charts** represent the sample mean of baseline process performance. Evaluate S Chart to verify stable common cause variation. **Xbar Chart** represents the sample standard deviation of the baseline process performance. Evaluate Xbar Chart for evidence of special causes. **Histogram with short term and long term variation**
Capability Indices	**Mean** is the sum of the values divided by the number of values. **Standard Deviation** shows how much variation or dispersion there is from the mean. A low standard deviation means that the population of data points is close to the mean, while a high standard deviation

	Components of a Baseline Performance Report
	means that the data is spread out over a large range of values.

DPMO Long Term measures the frequency of defects, as seen by the customer. The customer feels the variation in the process.

ZBench Short Term is centered artificially at the center of the tolerance and has a variation that is related to the pooled ("average") standard deviation of all the sub-groups. This represents the best the process could do if the process was centered and everything in the process was held as constant as possible. |
| **Process Benchmarks** | Defects per Million Opportunities (for defects) – DPMO – values are based on the estimates of the process variation and process mean. Initially, DPMO values may vary until the process and sub-groups within the process stabilize. Once you have collected enough data points, the DPMO should stabilize and you will be able to fully trust the Performance Report. |
| **Process Demographics** | Process demographics are characteristics of the process that help identify the process area, scope, specifications, and opportunities. Possible data elements for process demographics include report date, report creator, process name, department name, project name, units, unique process characteristics, lower and upper specification limits, and process opportunity descriptions. |
| **Process Capability** | **Potential (ST) Capability** shows the process perfectly centered, with short term (within sub-group) variation. The process tolerance is defined as ±3 short term standard deviations from the center of the specs. Process tolerance fits nicely between specifications.

Actual (LT) Capability shows the process centered on its mean (not perfectly centered) with long term (within sub-group and between sub-group) variation. Process tolerance is the same as with short term capability. |

Process Kaizen

Examples of Baseline Performance Reports

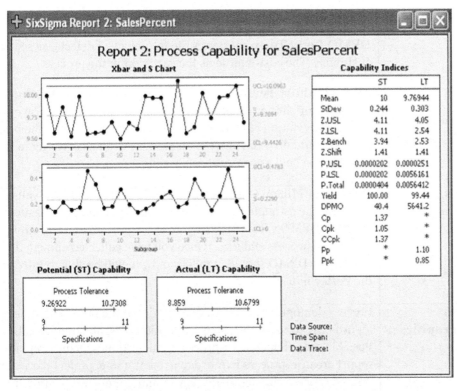

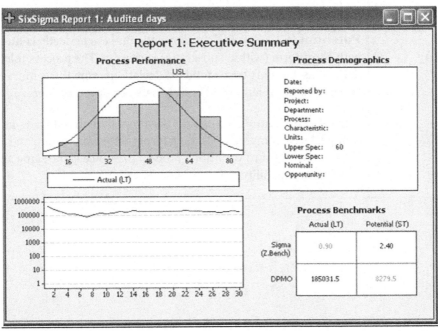

1.07 Prioritize Opportunities

Overview

During the Prioritize Opportunities activity, the Kaizen Facilitator reviews all of the possible process improvement opportunities in the project pipeline and determines the opportunities to move forward into charter development. Kaizen Events can be prioritized using the project selection checklist combined with improvement estimates for quality, cost, or speed.

Objective

- Understand the shifting and competing priorities within the business
- Assess the opportunity based on critical to selection criteria
- Establish the business reward for completing and business penalty for not completing
- Sort priorities based on above criteria and quality/cost/speed improvement estimates.

Estimated Time to Complete

15 to 90 Minutes

Inputs (Resources required by the process)	Where/From
Kaizen Facilitator	You
Project Team Member(s)	Organization
Prioritizing Kaizen Opportunities	Figure 1.07.01
Conference Room	Organization

Outputs (Deliverables from the process)	Possible Metrics
Prioritized Kaizen Event Pipeline	Number of Prioritized Events
Assigned Opportunity	Number of Activities Opportunities

Steps to Complete

1. Assess the opportunity based on critical to selection criteria

2. Establish the business reward for completing and business penalty for not completing

3. Sort priorities based on above criteria and quality/cost/speed improvement estimates.

4. Assign the opportunity for Charter Development

Process Kaizen

Figure 1.07.01 – Prioritizing Kaizen Opportunities

Filter 1 – Project Selection Criteria Checklist

Answer the following set of selection criteria questions, before establishing business reward, business penalty, and estimated benefits.

1. **Has the project been done already (or in progress)?**

   We don't want to "take credit" for a project that has been completed. Additionally, if an improvement effort is underway, one would have to determine if the Kaizen Event would be a better fit. If a Kaizen Event has been completed previously for this opportunity, the recommended approach should include:

   a. Review the deliverables and improvements from the previous Kaizen Event
   b. Validate the implemented improvements within the process and work area
   c. Determine possible leveragability in other sections or segments of the organization
   d. Review recommended actions that were not implemented during the Kaizen Event and determine Business Reward and Penalty for the improvement item
   e. Determine which improvement items should be immediately implemented
   f. Drive those improvements to completion (without completing another Kaizen Event for that area)
   g. Track results and continue to take corrective action as needed.

2. **Is there a pre-determined solution to the project goals?**

   This is referred to as a "just do it" project. If we (truly) know the solution, we do not need to apply a Kaizen Event and the required resources.

3. **Does the project conflict with other projects?**

   We want to ensure that by solving one problem, we do not worsen a related or non-related process (the law of unintended consequences). Often a secondary metric can be used to monitor the "other" desired process outcomes.

4. **Does the project have a high probability of success?**

   If we feel comfortable with all elements of the Project Selection Checklist, it is likely the project will be successful.

5. **Is project linked/aligned to goals of the business?**

   Kaizen is all about improving business performance – therefore, we will focus projects on those items which are important to business leaders. All projects should have line-of-sight to business unit goals. The CT flow down is a key tool to drive this linkage.

6. Does the cost reduction opportunity meet the goals of the business?

The project financials need to meet specific goals and guidelines developed by the business. Any deviations to these goals are to be approved prior to project initiation.

7. Has the project been properly scoped?

Project scope is one of the largest challenges of project selection. Consider the elements in the Project Selection Checklist when scoping the project (cost reduction opportunity, functional control, etc.). Ideally, the Project Sponsors conduct initial data analysis and high level mapping to drive the proper scope. Regardless of these efforts, the scope can change during project chartering and process definition.

8. Can starting points and end points for the process be defined?

This indicates what is within the scope of the project and what is not and also helps to visualize the process at a high level

9. Does the Project Sponsor have functional control of the impacted processes?

It is critical that the Project Sponsor have functional control of the impacted process both to influence and "connect" with impacted stakeholders as well as ensure the solutions will work well in the business. When Project Sponsors do not have functional control, the probability of success is minimized. Larger scoped, cross business unit projects are best led by the senior business leader responsible for all impacted areas.

10. Is data available on the Primary Metric (Y), or could it be developed quickly at a low cost)?

Kaizen Events use data to make decisions. If data is not available on the Primary Metric, the element you are trying to improve (cycle time, number of injuries, etc.) – you must determine the following: 1) how difficult it will be to obtain data; and 2) at what cost could you obtain the data? If the answer is relatively easy and inexpensive, proceed. If not, you should "park" the project until such data is available.

11. Is data collection relatively easy?

Some data is easily obtainable, and some is not. You must determine for your project how easily data can be gathered and analyzed. This is not to say you should not proceed with projects where data collection is difficult, but rather that you must assess how much effort it will take to collect the data, as no Kaizen Event can be successful without the necessary information.

12. Is there a "good" measurement system in place for the Primary Metric (Y)?

You know that Kaizen Events require data. Now ask yourself, "How good is the data? How much error is in the data?" This assessment is important because often times a Kaizen Facilitator needs to improve the measurement system prior to thoroughly deep diving and analyzing critical factors in the process. Although your assessment at this point is non-scientific, the Kaizen Events can use statistical analysis to validate the measurement system once a Kaizen Event is active.

13. Are resources available and supportive of this project (Project Sponsor/Process Owner, Team, etc.)?

A Kaizen Facilitator cannot succeed alone; they are the team leader "armed" with the Kaizen Event toolset and require a solid, supportive Project Sponsor/Process Owner and team. It is the responsibility of the Project Sponsor to define and communicate the project business case to the team.

14. Can you define the defects in the process?

Kaizen is a process targeted at eliminating waste, streamlining the process, and optimizing value added activities. It is, therefore, critical to define the wastes and defects in a process. In many parts of our business, we have not established defect definitions and "specifications." The Project Sponsor and Kaizen Facilitator need these definitions in order to calculate a baseline and establish improvement targets

Filter 2 – Estimated Reward vs. Estimated Penalty

Next, estimate the business reward should we realize this opportunity and the business penalty for not pursuing the opportunity. The default thought of most process owners and project sponsors is that everything is important. Kaizen Facilitators need to understand that there must be priorities.

Business Reward: Use the value of business reward (scale of 1-10) to determine the impact of implementing the improvement.

Business Penalty: Use the value of business penalty (scale of 1-10) to determine the impacts of not implementing the improvement. Remember, as a component of risk management there is always the option to do nothing- how much risk to we introduce into the process if we do nothing?

Filter 3 – Estimated Quality, Cost, or Time Benefits

Finally, estimate the quality, cost, and/or time benefits associated with the Kaizen Event goal.

Quality Benefits: Quality metrics are related directly to the customer's requirements on the outputs of your process – especially the final product. Quality metrics should have upper and lower specification limits and be monitored and controlled through statistical process control.

Cost Benefits: Cost of Poor Quality involves all the costs associated with providing poor quality products or services. There are four categories: internal failure costs (costs associated with defects found before the customer receives the product or service), external failure costs (costs associated with defects found after the customer receives the product or service), appraisal costs (costs incurred to determine the degree of conformance to quality requirements) and prevention costs (costs incurred to keep failure and appraisal costs to a minimum).

Time Benefits: Primary time metrics include process and activity times and lag times. Process and activity times can often be converted into labor dollars, while process lag and wait times can be attributed directly to the end stakeholder experience of the effort and duration of the process.

Process Kaizen

2. Charter Project

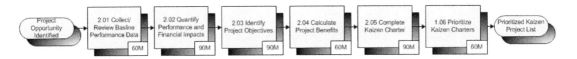

Overview

During the Charter Project sub-process, the Kaizen Facilitator and/or Project Sponsor collects, reviews and verifies baseline performance data, quantifies the performance and financial impacts of the opportunity, and develops a standard Kaizen Event project charter, including project objectives and estimated benefits. Kaizen Event project charters are then used to prioritize, select and assign Kaizen Event opportunities based on the organization's project selection criteria.

Objective

- Validate performance data and gather gaps in time period data
- Quantify performance opportunities and translate into financial benefit
- Charter prioritized opportunities
- Prioritize and assign Kaizen Events

2.01 Collect/Review Baseline Performance Data

Overview

During the Collect/Review Baseline Performance Data activity, the Kaizen Facilitator reviews any baseline data gathered during the Identify Opportunities sub-process. The Kaizen Facilitator may also be required to collect more baseline data to fill in gaps in time periods or to collect more details on the baseline performance. At this time, the Kaizen Facilitator also compares baseline process performance with established goals and objectives for the process area. Gaps between performance and plan are quickly validated prior to going to the Quantify Performance and Financial Impacts activity.

Objective

- Assess the usability and reliability of data and data sources
- Validate the Baseline Performance Report
- Gather any gaps in period data or data details

Estimated Time to Complete

15 to 120 Minutes

Inputs (Resources required by the process)	Where/From
Kaizen Facilitator	You
Baseline Performance Report	1.06 Establish Baseline Performance Activity
Assigned Opportunity	1.07 Prioritize Opportunities Activity
Opportunity Baseline Data	1.02 Establish Measures and Baseline Activity
Data Systems	Data Sources
Data Collection Plan	1.02 Establish Measures and Baseline Activity

Outputs (Deliverables from the process)	Possible Metrics
Validated/Updated Baseline Data	Number of Data Points, Data Time Period; Ease of Data Collection; Expense of Data Collection
Validated/Updated Baseline Performance Report	Gap between performance reports, changes in performance

Steps to Complete

1. Verify that all baseline data points are present and accounted for in Baseline Data

2. Collect any gaps in baseline data from data sources

3. Identify any other data sources that may hold similar data for comparison analysis

4. Compare data sources (if necessary)

5. Update the Baseline Performance Report with complete baseline data

6. Identify gaps and variance in performance to plan/expectations/process entitlement

2.02 Quantify Performance and Financial Impacts

Overview

During the Quantify Performance and Financial Impacts activity, the Kaizen Facilitator validates the short term and long term performance capability for the process and quantifies the financial impact of current performance, if possible. A problem or opportunity statement is drafted based on the quantification of current state performance and short term and long term possibilities for improvement. Baseline Data and the Baseline Performance Report (if completed) can be used to help provide a narrative description of the problem or opportunity.

Objective

- Quantify current performance relative to customer or organization expectations
- Identify the financial impact of current performance
- Provide a concise, well-defined statement of the issue

Estimated Time to Complete

15 to 90 Minutes

Inputs (Resources required by the process)	Where/From
Baseline Data	2.01 Collect/Review Baseline Performance Data
Baseline Performance Report	2.01 Collect/Review Baseline Performance Data
Kaizen Facilitator	You
Determining Process Capability	Figure 2.02.01
Performance Requirements	Process Owner; 1.06 Establish Baseline Performance

Inputs (Resources required by the process)	Where/From
Financial Requirements	Process Owner; Translation of Metrics into Financial benefits

Outputs (Deliverables from the process)	Possible Metrics
Problem/Opportunity Statement	Data included in narrative description of problem?
Estimate range of performance improvement	% Range of Improvement Opportunity
Estimated range of financial benefit	Return on Kaizen Investment

Steps to Complete

1. Describe the defect – How is the problem measured and what is the specific problem?

2. Describe the performance timeframe – When does this problem occur and how long has it persisted?

3. Describe the magnitude of the problem – What is the performance gap and what are the financial impacts?

4. Describe the current conditions – Under what situations does this problem occur and where does it occur (everyone or just some locations)?

Figure 2.02.01 – Determining Process Capability

Understanding Process Capability

Process Capability is the measurement of the capability for a process to deliver product or services that meet the needs of the customer as defined by the product or service specifications. It answers the question "How well is the process performing relative to customer expectations?"

Other ways to frame the questions that Process Capability answers are:

- How is the process currently performing?
- How well could the process perform?
- What can be expected tomorrow, next week, next month?
- Are our customers' expectations being met?

Process Capability allows you to:

1. Establish baseline performance measures for any process
2. Quantify how well a process could perform
3. Predict the frequency in failing to meet customer expectations
4. Diagnose the condition of the process
5. Determine high level objectives for process improvement
6. Monitor the impacts of process improvement efforts

Process Capability is a function of the data type (discrete vs. continuous) and the presence of rational sub-groups to help account for short-term and long-term variation in the process. Ultimately with Process Capability the process is characterized by the data it generates.

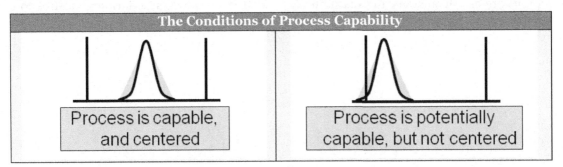

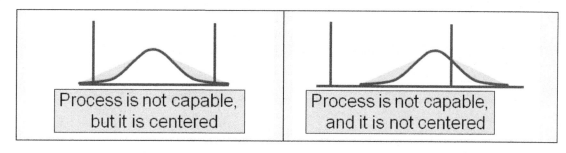

A stable process is one where the process mean and the process variation do not change dramatically over time. Instability is usually caused by a change in the process input, which in turn causes a change in the process output (mean and/or variation). If a process is not stable, we may be able to measure its capability today, but we will not be able to predict with confidence what the capability will be tomorrow. If you identify an unstable process, STOP and examine the inputs! You will most likely find significant variations in one or multiple input variables.

2.03 Identify Project Objectives

Overview

During the Identify Project Objectives activity, the Kaizen Facilitator and/or Process Owner create smart, measurable, attainable, reasonable, time-based (SMART) objectives for the Kaizen Event. An average Kaizen Event will yield 5-30% improvements in performance, so that is one option when first identifying Kaizen improvements.

Objective

- Establish clear project boundaries aligned with the Problem Statement
- Have an end goal or target in mind (but put actual improvement targets in Charter Goal section)

Estimated Time to Complete

5 to 15 Minutes

Inputs (Resources required by the process)	Where/From
Kaizen Facilitator	You
Problem Statement	2.02 Quantify Performance and Financial Impacts
Baseline Data	2.01 Collect/Review Baseline Performance Data
Baseline Performance Report	2.01 Collect/Review Baseline Performance Data

Estimate range of performance improvement	2.02 Quantify Performance and Financial Impacts
Estimated range of financial benefit	2.02 Quantify Performance and Financial Impacts

Outputs (Deliverables from the process)	Possible Metrics
Kaizen Event Objectives	Number of Objectives
Drafted Improvement Targets for Charter Goal	Proposed % of Improvement

Steps to Complete

1. Based on the estimated range of performance improvement, select a realistic improvement target

2. Create 3-7 bulleted objectives based on Kaizen Event standard work and the desired end state of performance

Figure 2.03.01 – Example Kaizen Event Project Objectives

Objectives:
- Define standard work based off best practices.
- Analyze and measure critical factors to why primary metric is underperforming
- Analyze and Measure the timings involved in the life cycle of the process
- Identify Failure Modes and Effects within the process and identify Critical to Quality characteristics.
- Develop an action plan for contingencies.
- Implement improvements (Change a controlled feature or process; Change a computer program or algorithm; train associates; repair or modify virtual/physical systems/environments)
- Report results

2.04 Calculate Project Benefits

Overview

During the Calculate Project Benefits activity, the Kaizen Facilitator takes the estimated improvement goals proposed for the Kaizen Event and determines the performance and financial benefits for the project. If the targeted metric is easily translated into dollars (e.g., inventory, square feet, labor, expenses, etc.), the Kaizen Facilitator calculates the financial savings based on the proposed improvement goal. Based on the results and predetermined charter selection criteria, the Kaizen Facilitator determines whether or not to move forward with chartering the project.

Objective

- Finalize the improvement goal based on the primary metric
- Translate the improvement goal into dollars whenever possible
- Measure the project benefits against predetermined selection criteria to determine chartering efforts

Estimated Time to Complete

30 to 120 Minutes

Inputs (Resources required by the process)	Where/From
Kaizen Facilitator	You
Kaizen Event Objectives	2.03 Identify Project Objectives
Drafted Improvement Targets for Charter Goal	2.03 Identify Project Objectives
Baseline Data	2.01 Collect/Review Baseline Performance Data
Financial Translation of Primary Metric	Process Owner; Kaizen Facilitator
Understanding Charter Selection Criteria Document	Figure 2.04.01
Problem/Opportunity Statement	2.02 Quantify Performance and Financial Impacts
Estimated Kaizen Event Costs	Kaizen Facilitator
Understanding the Costs of Kaizen Events	Figure 2.04.01

Outputs (Deliverables from the process)	Possible Metrics
Estimated Kaizen Event Performance Benefits	% Improvement
Estimated Kaizen Event Financial Benefits	$; ROI
Ready for Kaizen Event Charter	# Approved
Deferred Kaizen Event Opportunity	# Deferred

Steps to Complete

1. Determine improvement goal based on drafted improvement targets

2. Translate improvement targets into financial benefits
3. Prioritize Kaizen Event opportunities using charter selection criteria
4. Communicate opportunities selected for charter development

Figure 2.04.01 – Understanding Charter Selection Criteria

Understanding Charter Selection Criteria

It's important to establish a rigorous selection project for Kaizen Events because Kaizen Events should be primarily focused on applying process improvement activities and resources to activities that support critical business objectives and the demands of the customer. Poor project identification and sloppy charter development and selection are the main reasons why process improvement projects fail within organizations. You want to maintain a healthy pipeline of opportunities that have supporting data and clear problem statements, objectives and goals so that the Kaizen Event team understands the scope and value of the event.

How to establish Selection Criteria

Operational Excellence Filter: We previewed the Operational Excellence filter previously in the Understanding Kaizen Opportunities section. This list of questions helps the Kaizen Facilitator verify some critical to success factors prior to scoping and chartering the Kaizen Event opportunity.

Project Selection Criteria Checklist	Yes	No
1. Has the project been done already (or in progress)?		☑
2. Is there a pre-determined solution to the project goals?		☑
3. Does this project conflict with other projects?		☑
4. Does this project have a high probability of success?	☑	
5. Is the project linked/aligned to the goals of the business?	☑	
6. Does the cost reduction opportunity meet the goals of the business?	☑	
7. Has the project been properly scoped?	☑	
8. Can starting and end points for the process be defined?	☑	
9. Does the sponsor have functional control of the impacted process?	☑	
10. Are metrics available or could they be developed quickly at low cost?	☑	
11. Is data collection relatively easy?	☑	
12. Is there a "good" measurement system in place?	☑	
13. Are resources available and supportive of the project?	☑	
14. Can you define the defect in the process?	☑	

Strategic Alignment Filter: To establish Selection Criteria based on Strategic Alignment, Identify each goal for the department or organization and determine its "weight" on a scale of 1-10 based on how important the goal is to the organization. Then for each

Kaizen Event opportunity, score the opportunity for its alignment to each of the documented goals. Sort the projects by the weighted total.

Strategic Goals Filter							
Goal	A	B	C	D	E	F	Weighted Total
Weight	(1-10)	(1-10)	(1-10)	(1-10)	(1-10)	(1-10)	
Project 1							
Project 2							
Project 3							

Economic Impact Filter: Depending on the organization, Kaizen Events may have a required minimum return on investment in order to approve and assign the valuable time and resources for the event. By understanding the average costs for Kaizen Event, Kaizen Facilitators can estimate and validate the costs for Kaizen Events and compare those costs to the estimated financial benefits to come up with an estimated Return on Investment of the Kaizen. Other organizations combine an assessment of hard dollar benefits with softer benefits to the organization like morale and quality.

Hard Savings

Hard Savings are defined as project benefits that allow for a given amount of business to be conducted at lower expense or higher profit levels. Hard Savings are also defined as project benefits that allow for **more** business to be conducted without any increase to expense levels—as compared to actual, historical figures. Hard Savings must be measurable, observable over time and expressed in dollars.
Examples of Hard Savings are:

- Reduced labor costs
- Reduced overtime hours
- Reduced utility bills
- Reduced insurance costs
- Increased Sales and Profits

In some instances, Hard Savings will not result in actual spending reductions but, instead, will result in reallocation of resources across the organization. Clearly, the complexity of savings calculations varies from the very simple to the very complex; thus, one must exercise great care in identifying the real benefits of improvement projects.

Examples of more complex Hard Savings estimates:

- Rework costs are reduced as a result of eliminating defects; however, the labor savings are reinvested in other activities, instead of being reflected as a cost reduction.
- Warehousing space requirements are reduced and the space is utilized by another activity, one which would have required the budgeted rental of **more** space from an external party (i.e., not just usage of an existing facility).

Soft Savings

Soft Savings are defined as project benefits that may result in additional benefits that are hard to quantify. Typically, Soft Savings represent improvements through (a) reduced time to market, (b) risk avoidance, (c) cost avoidance, (d) improved employee morale, e) increased customer satisfaction and (f) an enhanced image for the organization

Specific examples of soft savings are:

- Improvements to customer or employee satisfaction.
- Labor savings related to productivity improvements that are less than one full-time equivalent (minimal)—unless overtime or outside contract labor is reduced.
- Warehousing space requirements are reduced, but we are neither able to vacate a facility nor are we able to sublet the space to another tenant.
- Improvements that do not immediately translate into savings due to contractual agreements preventing a reduction in costs.

Questions to ask for Financial Criteria Selection
1. Will the Kaizen Event improvements result in hard savings?
2. How much and when will the Kaizen Event deliver the expected savings?
3. Are there any costs associated with the implementation of the Kaizen Event?

Understanding the Costs of Kaizen Events

For most organizations Kaizen is a low-cost process improvement methodology where the primary spend is in time. Kaizen Events require groups of 5-8 subject matter experts, so the time of those people is required for the entire weeklong event. Labor is the main cost, but these people would have been working anyway and throughout the year they would have been expected to improve their processes to gain efficiencies and save money. In fact, organizations should dedicate 10-20% of employee time to improving processes.

To calculate the financial impact for your Kaizen Event:

1. Determine the Labor costs for the Kaizen Event
2. Determine costs for supplies needed for the Kaizen Event
3. Determine the cost of food and beverages
4. Determine the financial benefit target for the Kaizen Event (calculate the annualized net benefit)

5. Subtract total Kaizen Event costs from the annualized net financial benefits
6. Determine if total annualized financial benefits after costs meets the ROI for your organization

Example Breakout - Traditional Costs for Kaizen Events
Labor: Kaizen Facilitator and 5-8 subject matter experts for 40+ hours (Average $5,200)
Office Supplies: Sticky Notes, Markers, White Boards with Markers, Projector, Screen, Conference Room (Average $50)
Food and Beverage: Working breakfasts and lunches and a celebration dinner; possible project team gifts (e.g., t shirt) (Average $1000)
Improvement Supplies: Supplies required for implementing visual management and controls and other improvements (Average $250)

Total Costs for Kaizen Event: $6,500

Minimum Target for Financial Benefits for Kaizen Events: $30,000 annualized savings

2.05 Draft Kaizen Charter

Overview

During the Draft Kaizen Charter activity, the Kaizen Facilitator finalizes the key project charter elements. The Kaizen Facilitator validates the final problem statement, Primary Metric and Defect Definition, Goals, and Objectives. The Kaizen Facilitator also works on identifying assumptions, risks and obstacles to the successful completion of the Kaizen Event and identifies the roles desired for Project Team Members and the potentially Impacted Teams based on the process area. The Kaizen Charter becomes the single source of truth for process performance, project scope, and targeted goals.

Objective

- Communicate the critical factors for selecting and prioritizing Kaizen Events
- Provide a clear description of the opportunity
- Back the opportunity with historical baseline data and performance analysis
- Create a single source of truth for project scope and objectives

Estimated Time to Complete

30 to 90 Minutes

Inputs (Resources required by the process)	Where/From
Kaizen Facilitator	You
Kaizen Event Objectives	2.03 Identify Project Objectives

Inputs (Resources required by the process)	Where/From
Drafted Improvement Targets for Charter Goal	2.03 Identify Project Objectives
Baseline Data	2.01 Collect/Review Baseline Performance Data
Understanding Project Selection Criteria Document	Figure 2.05.01
Problem/Opportunity Statement	2.02 Quantify Performance and Financial Impacts
Estimated Kaizen Event Costs	Kaizen Event Cost Worksheet
Estimated Kaizen Event Performance Benefits	2.02 Quantify Performance and Financial Impacts
Estimated Kaizen Event Financial Benefits	2.02 Quantify Performance and Financial Impacts
Project Team – Desired Roles	Process Owner; Kaizen Facilitator; Project Sponsor
Impacted Team(s)	Process Owner; Kaizen Facilitator; Project Sponsor; External teams
Assumptions, Risks and Obstacles	Process Owner; Kaizen Facilitator; Project Sponsor; External teams

Outputs (Deliverables from the process)	Possible Metrics
Kaizen Event Charter	# of Charters; Total Estimated Financial Benefit of Charters

Steps to Complete

1. Open the Kaizen Event Charter Template
2. Document the Problem/Opportunity using data to back up the narrative
3. Document the Primary Metric and defect definition for that metric
4. Document your vision of what success looks like for the Kaizen Event
5. Document the targeted performance goal
6. Document the objectives to be accomplished during the Kaizen Event
7. Document any criteria critical for success of the Kaizen Event

8. Document Assumptions, Risks and Obstacles that may prevent the Kaizen Event from being a success

9. Document the desired team roles and the potentially impacted teams related to the process area

Figure 2.05.01 - Understanding a Kaizen Project Charter

The project charter is a document that summarizes the information derived from project identification and scoping and provides justification for project selection.

\	Understanding Kaizen Event Project Charters
Purpose	• Assures that the Team and Senior Management understand and agree on the problem, scope and objective of the project
Importance	• Ensures that the project supports organizational strategy • Prevents misunderstanding
Results	• Focused efforts • Appropriate resource and organizational support • Enhanced project success

The Project Charter is established by the Project Sponsor and signed by the Project Sponsor and Kaizen Facilitator.

\	Primary Elements of a Kaizen Event Project Charter
Problem/Opportunity Statement	The purpose and function of a problem/opportunity statement is to quantify the current performance of the process relative to customer expectations. It is important to identify the financial impact of current performance and provide a concise, well defined statement of the issue.
Primary Metric and Defect Definition	The primary metric is traditionally the key performance indicator for the process outputs. Kaizen Facilitators should document the operational definition of the metrics (understand when and how metrics are measured) and be able to link the metric to the project goal and identify a defect in performance.
Goal	An average Kaizen Event will yield a 10-50% improvement in performance
Objectives	Project Objectives should be specific, measurable, attainable, reasonable, and time based (also known as SMART). Kaizen

Primary Elements of a Kaizen Event Project Charter	
	Facilitators should create project objectives based on clear project boundaries, specific Kaizen Event deliverables and milestones, which should also support the project goal.
Team Resources	It is important to identify the roles and responsibilities and resources required to successfully improve process performance. Project Sponsors and Kaizen Facilitators should not only identify the required resources, but also identify impacted cross-functional teams.
Assumptions, Risks, and Obstacles	**Assumptions** are propositions established because all the facts are not yet available. Assumptions should be a proposition or assertion about some characteristic of the future that underlies the current operations or plans of the organization. **Risks** are the potential threats or opportunities to the success of the Kaizen Event. As risks are identified, probability is usually attributed to the risk and a reaction plan is developed in case the risk occurs. **Obstacles** are immediate issues or impediments identified that will need to be resolved before successfully pursuing the Kaizen Event. When obstacles are identified a plan of action should be developed to immediately remove or work through the obstacle.

With a written Charter, the expectations of both parties are known, and by their joint signatures, the Kaizen Facilitator and Project Sponsor have:

- Validated the importance of the project
- Committed themselves to the project's success
- Identified the goals and objectives of the project
- Scoped the opportunity and identified the right resources

Figure 2.05.02 – Kaizen Event Project Charter Template

Kaizen Event Project Charter Template

Process Kaizen

Kaizen Event Overview Statement (why, what & when; not how)	**Project Name:**	**Project Source:** *(Planning, Kaizen, External, Internal, Management, Just Do It)*	**Project Manager(s) & Sponsor(s):** *(Who wants this and who is going to manage)*

Problem/Opportunity:
(Why)
Problem Statements should include:
- *Description of the defect*
  - *What specifically is the problem?*
  - *How is the problem measured?*
- *Time Frame*
  - *When does the problem occur?*
  - *How long has it persisted?*
- *Magnitude of the problem*
  - *What is the performance gap?*
  - *Include financial impact*
- *Conditions*
  - *Under what situations does the problem occur?*
  - *Where does the problem occur (some locations more than others, everywhere)?*

Primary Metric and Defect Definition
(How is the output measured and what is failure)
Primary Metric:
- *Description of project measurement*
- *Directly related to the project defect*
- *Directly related to the project objective*
- *Include Units of Measure*
- *Know the Operational Definition of the metric*
- *Understand how the project is to be measured*
- *Example: Delivery of product to customer*
- *We measure when the product leaves shipping*
- *Customer measures when it arrives on their dock*

Defect Definition:
- *A defect is unacceptable performance*
- *It must be aligned with the Problem Statement and Project Objective*
- *It must be CONCISE*

Goal:
(What)
(link Department and/or Team goals and Principles)

Kaizen Event Project Charter Template			
Kaizen Event Overview Statement (why, what & when; not how)	**Project Name:**	**Project Source:** (Planning, Kaizen, External, Internal, Management, Just Do It)	**Project Manager(s) & Sponsor(s):** (Who wants this and who is going to manage)
Objectives: (What, When) (is there a date it must be delivered or would like to be delivered on ?) *Success should be:* <ul><li>*based on clear project boundaries*</li><li>*have an end goal or target that is benchmarked against other areas of the company or the industry*</li><li>*achievable in 4-6 months*</li><li>*aligned with Problem Statement*</li></ul>			
Success Criteria / Value: (Value) (IRACIS – Increased Revenue or Avoided Costs or Improved Services)			
Assumptions, Risks, Obstacles:			
Impacted Teams: (what teams will have to do the work or be affected by the deliverables)			
Prepared By:	**Date:**	**Approved By:**	**Date:**

2.06 Prioritize Kaizen Charters

Overview

During the Prioritize Kaizen Charters activity, the same selection criteria and logic are applied as were applied in selecting an opportunity for chartering. The Kaizen Facilitator takes the final estimates for project benefits and filters the project charter through the Operational Excellence filter, Strategic Alignment filter, and Financial Impact filter.

Objective

- Apply standard project selection criteria to all Kaizen Event Charters
- Select and assign the best project opportunities
- Efficiently manage process improvement resources

Estimated Time to Complete

10 to 90 Minutes

Inputs (Resources required by the process)	Where/From
Kaizen Facilitator	You
Project Sponsor; Process Owners	Organization
Other Process Improvement Stakeholders	Organization
Project Charter(s)	2.05 Draft Kaizen Charter
Project Selection Criteria	2.04.01 Understanding Project Selection Criteria

Outputs (Deliverables from the process)	Possible Metrics
Assigned Kaizen Event	Number of Assigned Kaizen Events
Prioritized Kaizen Event Pipeline	Number of Prioritized Kaizen Events

Steps to Complete

1. Establish Operational Excellence filter and apply selection criteria checklist.

2. Apply established strategic alignment filter and apply selection criteria values

3. Apply established financial criteria filters

4. Apply appropriate value weighting and determine final selection criteria values

5. Sort projects based on final selection criteria values

Figure 2.06.01 – Understanding Project Selection Criteria

Understanding Project Selection Criteria (Copied from Figure 2.04.01)

Process Kaizen

It's important to establish a rigorous selection project for Kaizen Events because Kaizen Events should be primarily focused on applying process improvement activities and resources to activities that support critical business objectives and the demands of the customer. Poor project identification and sloppy charter development and selection are the main reasons process improvement projects fail within organizations. You want to maintain a healthy pipeline of opportunities that have supporting data and clear problem statements, objectives and goals so that the Kaizen Event team understands the scope and value of the event.

How to establish Selection Criteria

Operational Excellence Filter: We previewed the Operational Excellence filter previously in the Understanding Kaizen Opportunities section. This list of questions helps the Kaizen Facilitator verify some critical to success factors prior to scoping and chartering the Kaizen Event opportunity.

Project Selection Criteria Checklist	Yes	No
1. Has the project been done already (or in progress)?		☑
2. Is there a pre-determined solution to the project goals?		☑
3. Does this project conflict with other projects?		☑
4. Does this project have a high probability of success?	☑	
5. Is the project linked/aligned to the goals of the business?	☑	
6. Does the cost reduction opportunity meet the goals of the business?	☑	
7. Has the project been properly scoped?	☑	
8. Can starting and end points for the process be defined?	☑	
9. Does the sponsor have functional control of the impacted process?	☑	
10. Are metrics available or could they be developed quickly at low cost?	☑	
11. Is data collection relatively easy?	☑	
12. Is there a "good" measurement system in place?	☑	
13. Are resources available and supportive of the project?	☑	
14. Can you define the defect in the process?	☑	

Strategic Alignment Filter: To establish Selection Criteria based on Strategic Alignment, Identify each goal for the department or organization and determine its "weight" on a scale of 1-10 based on how important the goal is to the organization. Then for each Kaizen Event opportunity, score the opportunity for its alignment to each of the documented goals.

Strategic Goals Filter							
Goal	A	B	C	D	E	F	Weighted Total
Weight	10	8	7	7	5	5	

Project 1							
Project 2							
Project 3							

Economic Impact Filter: Depending on the organization, Kaizen Events may have a required minimum return on investment in order to approve and assign the valuable time and resources for the event. By understanding the average costs for Kaizen Event, Kaizen Facilitators can estimate and validate the costs for Kaizen Events and compare those costs to the estimated financial benefits to come up with an estimated Return on Investment of the Kaizen. Other organizations combine an assessment of hard dollar benefits with softer benefits to the organization like morale and quality.

Understanding the Costs of Kaizen Events

For most organizations Kaizen is a low-cost process improvement methodology where the primary spend is in time. Kaizen Events require groups of 5-8 subject matter experts, so the time of those people are required for the entire weeklong event. Labor is the main cost, but these people would have been working anyway and throughout the year they would have been expected to improve their processes to gain efficiencies and save money. In fact, organizations should dedicate 10-20% of employee time to improving processes.

To calculate the financial impact for your Kaizen Event:

1. Determine the Labor costs for the Kaizen Event
2. Determine costs for supplies needed for the Kaizen Event
3. Determine the cost of food and beverages
4. Determine the financial benefit target for the Kaizen Event (calculate the annualized net benefit)
5. Subtract total Kaizen Event costs from the annualized net financial benefits
6. Determine in total annualized financial benefits after costs meets the ROI for your organization

Example Breakout - Traditional Costs for Kaizen Events

Labor: Kaizen Facilitator and 5-8 subject matter experts for 40+ hours (Average $5,200)
Office Supplies: Sticky Notes, Markers, White Boards with Markers, Projector, Screen, and Conference Room (Average $50)
Food and Beverage: Working breakfasts and lunches and a celebration dinner; possible project team gifts (e.g., t shirt) (Average $1000)
Improvement Supplies: Supplies required for implementing visual management and controls and other improvements (Average $250)

Total Traditional Costs for Kaizen Event: $6,500

Minimum Target for Financial Benefits for Kaizen Events: $30,000 annualized savings

3. Kickoff Project

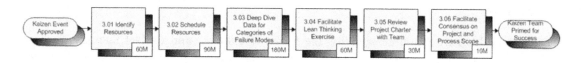

Overview

During the Kickoff Project sub-process, the Kaizen Facilitator and/or Project Sponsor work to identify resources for project team members, manage the logistics of the Kaizen Event, and schedule resources. The Kaizen Facilitator also performs "deep dives" on baseline data and identifies categories of failure modes based on failure modes effects analysis of a random population of defect data. Finally, the Kaizen Facilitator coordinates a Lean Thinking exercise to get the project team primed from focused Lean improvements, reviews the project charter with the team, and ultimately builds consensus on the process and the project scope.

Objective

- Identify and commit resources to the project
- Get the right people in the room at the right time
- Provide initial analysis into performance failure modes
- Transfer Lean thinking knowledge and Kaizen Event plan

3.01 Identify Resources

Overview

During the Identify Resources activity, the Kaizen Facilitator and Project Sponsor/Process Owner work together to identify the appropriate Kaizen Event team members based on the roles required to improve the process area. Kaizen Event team members are primarily subject matter experts in the process area and are the people who do the work. Other less frequent Kaizen Event team members include leads, managers, stakeholders, and external team members. Cross-functional subject matter experts that influence the process area should be included as Kaizen Event team members.

Objective

- Quickly identify the right people to bring together for the effort
- Determine resource availability and begin to commit
- Communicate urgency and important of Kaizen Event

Estimated Time to Complete

5 to 30 Minutes

Inputs (Resources required by the process)	Where/From
Kaizen Facilitator	You
Project Sponsor/Process Owner	Organization
Project Charter	2.05 Draft Kaizen Charter
Process Area	Project Charter
Cross-Functional or Impacted Teams/Stakeholders	Project Charter

Outputs (Deliverables from the process)	Possible Metrics
Kaizen Event Team Members Identified	Number of Team Members
Resources Committed	Level of Commitment; Time Commitment; Dates Available
General Timeframe Established	Date Range; # of Days until window of opportunity

Steps to Complete

1. Review the Desired Project Team Roles on Project Charter

2. Select high performing subject matter experts to meet requirements of the team roles

3. Identify general timeframe of window of opportunity and negotiate availability and commitment

3.02 Schedule Resources

Overview

During the Schedule Resource activity, the Kaizen Facilitator and Project Sponsor/Process Owner finalize the dates for the Kaizen Event and formally invite the Kaizen Event Team Members for the weeklong even. The Kaizen Facilitator tracks who accepts and who declines the invitation and identifies new resources or escalates as needed.

Objective

- Clearly communicate the expectations and timeframe for the Kaizen Event
- Make sure the right people are invited and accept the Kaizen Event invitation
- Communicate expectations for the Kaizen Event and share the Kaizen Event Charter

Estimated Time to Complete

5 to 120 Minutes

Inputs (Resources required by the process)	Where/From
Kaizen Facilitator	You
Identified Kaizen Event Team Member	3.01 Identify Resources
Project Sponsor/Process Owner	Organization
Kaizen Event Charter	2.05 Draft Kaizen Charter
Email/Phone	Technology
Conference Room Availability	Facilities
Projector Availability	Technology
Kaizen Event Team Member Availability	Calendar
General Kaizen Event Timeframe Established	Kaizen Facilitator
Kaizen Event Team Directory Communication Sheet Template	Figure 3.02.01

Outputs (Deliverables from the process)	Possible Metrics
Scheduled Kaizen Event	Number of Scheduled Kaizen Events
Kaizen Event Invitation	Number of Invitations Sent
Informed Kaizen Event Team Member	Number of Invitations Accepted; Number

	of Invitations Declined

Steps to Complete

1. Review identified team members and verify contact information

2. Develop Kaizen Event Team Member Communication Sheet

3. Verify the general Kaizen Event timeline and window of opportunity with Project Sponsor/Process Owner

4. Develop and send Kaizen Event meeting invite (5 Day, 40+ hour all week event).

5. Track accepted and declined invitation and move Kaizen Event schedule as needed. Should only move date twice – and do so reluctantly

Figure 3.02.01 - Kaizen Event Team Directory Communication Sheet Template

Kaizen Event Team Directory

Name	Role	Title	Phone	Email	Manager	Comments	Identified	Priority	Confirmed
				-					
				-					
				-					
				-					
				-					
				-					
				-					
				-					

3.03 Deep Dive Data for Categories of Failure Modes

Overview

During the Deep Dive Data for Categories of Failure Modes activity the Kaizen Facilitator selects a random population of data which are considered defects and analyzes the way the defect occurred (i.e., how the input went wrong), the impact on the customer (internal or external), and the possible causes for the input going bad. The Kaizen Facilitator then categorizes the analysis into 3-7 key failure modes and presents the analysis to the project team a couple weeks prior to the Kaizen Event.

Objective

- Categorize initial analysis of failure modes for defect data
- Provide the project team glimpses into areas of opportunity
- Communicate what the data is telling us

Estimated Time to Complete

240 to 2400 Minutes

Inputs (Resources required by the process)	Where/From
Kaizen Facilitator	You
Baseline Data	2.01 Collect/Review Baseline Performance Data
Random Sample of Defect Data	Baseline Data
Establishing Risk and Confidence Intervals	Figure 3.03.01
Failure Modes Effects Analysis Template	Figure 3.04.02
Defect Audit Information	Production/Historical Information

Outputs (Deliverables from the process)	Possible Metrics
Failure Modes of Effects of Defect Data	Number of Instances analyzed
Categories of Failure Modes	3-7 categories of Failure
Possible Causes for Failures	Identified causes of failure

Steps to Complete

1. Identify defects in baseline data based on defect definition of primary metric

2. Determine your level of confidence required for establishing failure modes (traditionally between 75-95%)

3. Determine the random population for deep dive based on total population and confidence level required

4. Research and analyze the specific failure modes, failure effects, and possible causes for each data point of the sample population (Categorize into 3-7 subsets of failure)

5. Summarize your research and analysis using the Pre-Kaizen Deep Dive Report

Figure 3.03.01 – Establishing Risk and Confidence Intervals

In statistics, Confidence Intervals are used to indicate the reliability of an estimate – in the case of deep diving baseline data it is our confidence level that the sample population of data represents the total population of baseline data points. Typically, we only want to be wrong between 10-15% of the time, so as a rule of thumb we want our confidence in being correct to be about 85-90%. This confidence level will ultimate determine the sample size necessary for your data. The confidence level tells you the reliability of your estimate. These confidence levels are closely related to statistical significance testing.

Take note that a claim of 95% confidence in something is normally taken as indicating virtual certainty. In statistics, a claim to 95% confidence simply means that the observer has seen something occur that happens only one time in 20 or less. If one were to roll two dice and get double six (which happens 1/36th of the time, or about 3%), few would claim that as proof that the dice were fixed, although statistically speaking one could have a 97% confidence that they were. Similarly, the finding of a statistical link at 95% confidence is NOT proof, nor even very good evidence, that there is any real connection between the things linked.

Remember, that confidence intervals are an expression of probability and are subject to the normal laws of probability. The principle behind confidence intervals was formulated to provide an answer to the question raise in statistical inference of how to deal with the uncertainty inherent in results derived from data that are themselves only a randomly selected subset of an entire statistical population of possible datasets. One alternative to confidence intervals is provided by Bayesian inference in the form of credible intervals.

For our purposes, 85-90% confidence in the sample data should be sufficient. We don't want the costs of data collection and data analysis to exceed to value delivered from a Kaizen Event.

Central Limit Theorem

In probability theory, the central limit theorem states conditions under which the mean of a sufficiently large number of independent random variables, each with finite mean and variance, will be approximately normally distributed. So, if a variable X has a distribution with mean = μ and standard deviation = σ, then the sampling distribution of X (its mean) having a sample size of n will have a mean of μ_x and a standard deviation of σ_x. The data will also tend to be normally distributed as the sample size becomes large. If you don't know your distributions then your sample size should be at least 30 and probably more.

Hypothesis Testing

When we take a sample of the data, we are looking to establish confidence in our analysis of the defects within the data. We want to be able to accept that the instances of the data analyzed accurately represent to population of defects within the data. Ultimately, you are communicating your level of confidence that the deep dive analysis into the defects is an accurate representation of the population of defects.

Sampling Examples

Sampling is used to select a subset of the population of data to estimate or infer characteristics of the population. This is used when you can't deep dive every instance of data in the population.

Simple Random Sampling 	<ul><li>Each "unit" has an equal chance of being selected</li><li>Simple</li><li>Unit = individual measure</li><li>Sub-group like units</li></ul> Example Scenario: To estimate the average height of the class, select 10 students at random. Calculate the average height of the sample.
Stratified Sampling 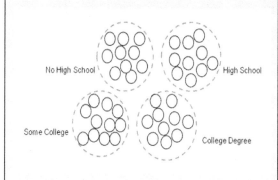	<ul><li>Researchers may elect to evaluate <u>mutually exclusive strata</u></li><li>Selecting individual units</li><li>Separate data by some factor (location, shift, product...)</li><li>Stratified random sampling: Random selection of individual units <u>within</u> strata</li><li>Useful when strata are expected to yield different results</li><li>Strata are suspected sources of variation</li><li>Unit = individual observation from</li></ul>

	each strata

Determining Sample Sizes based on how confident you need to be in your assessment

A sample is a portion or subset of units taken from a population of data of measured characteristics. Sample size determination is the act of choosing the number of observations to include in a statistical sample. Sample size is important to your deep dive activities because the Kaizen Facilitator will be making inferences about the total population of baseline data based on the sample population. Sample sizes are traditionally determined based on the expense of data collection and the need to have sufficient confidence in the sample size.

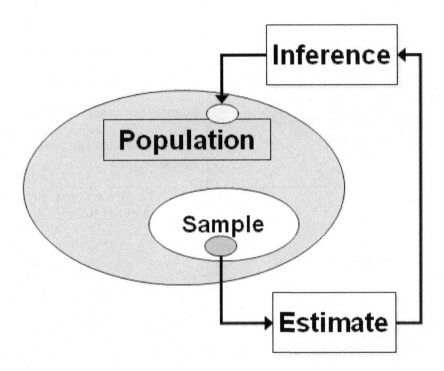

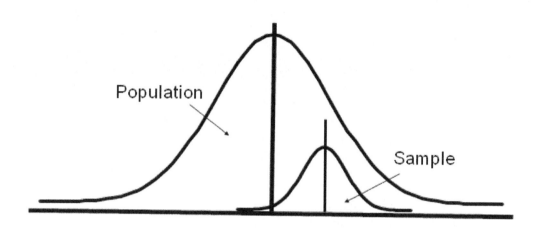

Sometimes, simple random sampling, as we use here, may result in a sample that doesn't reflect the makeup of the population. For instance, a simple random sample of 20 people from an organization will on average produce ten men and ten women, but in any given trial one gender is likely to be overrepresented and the other underrepresented. Systematic and stratified techniques attempt to overcome this problem by using information about the population to choose a more representative sample.

Systematic sampling relies on arranging the total population according to some ordering scheme and then selecting elements at regular intervals through that ordered list.

Prior to gathering the Kaizen Event team members, it is often a good idea to analyze defects data to determine common failure mode themes. By selecting and analyzing a random sample of defects data, the Kaizen Facilitator may be able to establish some of the most common failure modes in the process. If the detailed supporting data is available to determine how and why the instance did not meet performance expectations, the Kaizen Facilitator should "deep dive" the dataset to provide the Kaizen Event team

During the pre-Kaizen Event Deep Dive, the Kaizen Event Facilitator uses a simplified Failure Modes Effects Analysis template to quickly document specific failure modes, failure effects, and possible causes for each data point of the sample population.

Figure 3.04.02 - Failure Modes Effects Analysis – Deep Dive Template

Defect Instance	Unique Identifier	Potential Failure Mode	Potential Failure Effects	Potential Causes	Actions Recommended

Defect Instance	Unique Identifier	Potential Failure Mode	Potential Failure Effects	Potential Causes	Actions Recommended
Number	What is the unique identifier for the instance?	In what ways did the instance go wrong? (Attempt to create 3-7 high level categories of failure)	What was the impact on the customer (internal or external)?	What caused the instance Input to go wrong?	What are the actions for reducing the occurrence of the Cause?
1					
2					
3					
4					

3.04 Facilitate Lean Thinking Exercise

Overview

This hands-on training and simulation is designed to enhance participants' knowledge and understanding of Lean Thinking through a hands-on simulation of Lean principles in action.

Objective

- Understand Lean Thinking
- Learn the components and activities for eliminating waste in processes
- Hands-on experience of traditional thinking and Lean thinking

Estimated Time to Complete

60 Minutes

Inputs (Resources required by the process)	Where/From

Process Kaizen

Kaizen Facilitator	You
Lego Brand Building Block Kit	You
Understanding Lean Thinking Handout	Figure 3.04.01
Exercise Production Tracker Spreadsheet	Figure 3.04.02
Stopwatch	You
3-5 Team Members	Organization or Project Team

Outputs (Deliverables from the process)	Possible Metrics
Understanding of Lean Methodology	Time to Review; Number of Questions; Time to Complete each Production Run

Steps to Complete

1. Provide a quick introduction to the Lean Thinking Exercise

2. Identify team roles and responsibilities within the exercise

    a. Material Handler(s) (1 Required Position; 1 Additional Optional Position)

    b. Operator A (Required Position)

    c. Operator B (Required Position)

    d. Shipper (Required Position)

    e. Quality Assurance (Optional)

    f. Accounting (Optional)

3. Provide job roles to each team member

4. Run First Production Simulation

5. Discuss and document production performance, what went well, what didn't go so well, and what the team would like to see done differently.

6. Hand out the Understanding Lean Thinking document

7. Prepare materials for Second Production Simulation

8. Set up and introduce the Lean improvements to the environment

9. Run Second Production Simulation

10. Discuss and document production performance, what went well, what didn't go so well, and what the team would like to see done differently.

Process Kaizen

Process Kaizen

Figure 3.04.01 – Facilitating a Lean Thinking Exercise

Run 1(Traditional Thinking):

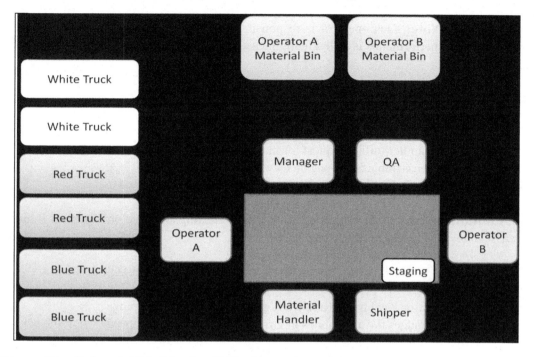

Run 1(Traditional Thinking): All blocks are in each operators bin mixed with other miscellaneous blocks. Bins should be filled to the top with blocks.

Material Handler: Sits between Operator A and Operator B
Operator A: Stands at table as far away from Operator B as possible.
Operator B: Sits at table
Shipper: Sits at table
Responsibilities of the Manager (Optional): The company pays suppliers $50 for each block and we pay each operator $200 per shift. The Manager is responsible for providing the manufacturing batch schedule, counting the number of blocks used at the end of a shift, counting the number of units produced at the end of a shift, and calculating the units sold in dollars, the cost of blocks, the cost of labor, and the overall profitability of the shift.
Responsibilities in QA (Optional): The Quality Assurance Manager observes the operations on the production floor and identified defects in the process. The Quality Assurance Manager pulls any unit or component in which an error or defect has been observed and keeps a tally of the number of defects and number of blocks in the defective unit or component.

Performance Goal: Usually we can make 10-12 block assemblies per shift. However, our new orders are for 30 assemblies per shift! 10 of each color. The organization does try to minimize change over and due to constant constraints on equipment, they like to make batches, although not always in the same size. Customers want the company to ship orders in groups of five as this is a full truckload and minimizes shipping costs.

Performance Note: Each operator is responsible for the performance in his or her area and operational performance is individually measured by how much work an operator gets done.

Order of Operations:
1. Operators A and B review production schedules
2. Operators A and B request materials from Material Handler
3. Material Handler fulfills request for materials
4. Operator A assembles an 8 peg block with a 4 peg block
5. Once Operator A makes a batch it goes to Operator B

Additional Operation: Color Change – Before starting a new color, Operator B must assemble 4 1x8 blocks of the appropriate color.

6. Operator B adds another 4 peg block and then completes assembly with a 2 peg block
7. Once Operator B completes a batch it goes to staging for shipping
8. Shipper arranges the assemblies in groups of five in the appropriate colored truck

Shift: An entire shift lasts 4 minutes!

Batch Scheduling:
Batch Order 1: 2 Reds; 4 Whites; 3 Blues
Batch Order 2: 1 Blue; 3 Reds; 2 Whites
Shipper Ships when Truck has 5 of a colored assembly

Run 1 Debrief: Ask for recommendations on how to improve operations. Quickly settle on organizing the workplace with 6S

Process Kaizen

Run 2(Lean Thinking):

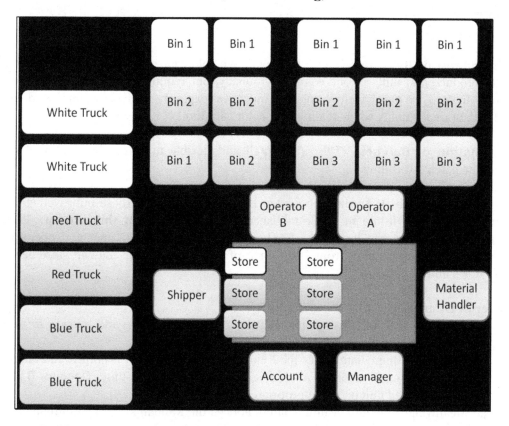

Run 2 (Pull Systems and Work Balance): Enhanced work instructions are used for each process. In addition to Blocks being organized by color and peg count at the work areas of both operators, a Kanban sheet is used for visual controls and pull scheduling. Both operators have enough blocks to make 20 units of each color.

Operator A: Stands at table
Operator B: Stands at table
Shipper: Stands at table

Responsibilities of the Manager (Optional): The company pays suppliers $50 for each block and we pay each operator $200 per shift. The Manager is responsible for providing the manufacturing batch schedule, counting the number of blocks used at the end of a shift, counting the number of units produced at the end of a shift, and calculating the units sold in dollars, the cost of blocks, the cost of labor, and the overall profitability of the shift.

Responsibilities in QA (Optional): The Quality Assurance Manager observes the operations on the production floor and identified defects in the process. The Quality Assurance Manager pulls any unit or component in which an error or defect has been observed and keeps a tally of the number of defects and number of blocks in the defective unit or component.

Performance Goal: Usually we can make 10-12 block assemblies per shift. However, our new orders are for 30 assemblies per shift! 10 of each color.

Elimination of the Changeover Process: We sold that old monolithic machine that could produce 500 units of one color very quickly, but required changeover for different colors. Instead, we now have two smaller (much less expensive!) machines that work faster and with more flexibility when dealing with color variations.

Elimination of Batches: The same small and flexible machines have allowed us to eliminate batch scheduling.

Setup for Next Shift: During the Kaizen Event that generated these improvements, we setup a Kanban environment and established the components for shift startup. Place a completed unit of each color on the Kanban store between the shipper and operator B. Place a complete component from Operator A of each color on the Kanban store between Operator B and Operator A.

Order of Operations:
1. Shipper takes one completed unit from Kanban store and moves it to the appropriate truck
2. Operator B immediately sees the Kanban store for that unit is empty, and takes the corresponding Component A and begins completing a new unit. Operator B places the completed unit on the appropriate Kanban store.
3. Meanwhile, Operator A immediately notices the Kanban store for Component A is empty and begins completing a new Component A of the appropriate color.

Shift: An entire shift lasts 4 minutes!

Run 2 Debrief: Ask for recommendations on how to improve operations.

Figure 3.04.02 – Lego Assembly Job Instruction Breakdown Sheets

JOB INSTRUCTION BREAKDOWN SHEET

Operation: Assemble Part A

Parts: 2X1 block (X10), 2x4 block (X10)

Tools and Materials: Part A Kanban Pad; 2X1 block storage container (one of each white, orange, blue); 2X4 block storage container (one of each white, orange, blue)

Important Steps	Key Points	Reasons
A logical segment of the operation when something happens to advance the work	Anything in a step that might… 1. Make or break the job 2. Injure the worker 3. Make the work easier to do, i.e., "knack," "trick," special timing, bit of special information.	Reasons for the key points.
1. Observe Kanban Pad	Closely monitor each color Kanban Pad for activity	To quickly respond to customer demand as a Part is taken from inventory
2. Observe Removal of Part A from Kanban Pad	Pay close attention to the color of the Part removed	To quickly start production of the correct color of Part A when it is in demand
3. Select 2X4 block	Use the correct color block based on the part removed from the Kanban Pad	Select the right materials the first time with no rework or errors
4. Select 2X1 block	Use the correct color block based on the part removed from Kanban Pad	Select the right materials the first time with no rework or errors
5. Secure 2X1 block to 2X4 block	Connect the 2X1 to one of the end of the 2X4 block	Build the right product the first time with no rework or errors
6. Place Part A on Kanban Pad	Place the part on the correct color Kanban Pad	Clearly communicate at a glance that the correct colored Part A is available

JOB INSTRUCTION BREAKDOWN SHEET

Operation: Assemble Part B

Parts: 2X3 block (X10)

Tools and Materials: Part A Inventory Kanban; Part B Kanban Pad; 2X3 block storage container (one of each white, orange, blue)

Important Steps	Key Points	Reasons
A logical segment of the operation when something happens to advance the work	Anything in a step that might... 1. Make or break the job 2. Injure the worker 3. Make the work easier to do, i.e., "knack," "trick," special timing, bit of special information.	Reasons for the key points.
1. Observe Kanban Pad	Closely monitor each color Kanban Pad for activity	To quickly respond to customer demand as a Part is taken from inventory
2. Observe Removal of Part B from Kanban Pad	Pay close attention to the color of the Part removed	To quickly start production of the correct color of Part B when it is in demand
3. Select Part A	Pick the correct color Part A based on the part removed from the Kanban Pad	Select the right materials the first time with no rework or errors
4. Select 2X3 block	Use the correct color block based on the part removed from Kanban Pad	Select the right materials the first time with no rework or errors
5. Secure 2X3 block to Part A	Connect the 2X3 to Part A so it forms one solid rectangular component	Build the right product the first time with no rework or errors
6. Place Part B on Kanban Pad	Place the part on the correct color Kanban Pad	Clearly communicate at a glance that the correct colored Part A is available

JOB INSTRUCTION BREAKDOWN SHEET

Operation: Assemble Final Product

Parts: 2X2 block (X10)

Tools and Materials: Part B Inventory Kanban; Part C Kanban Pad; 2X2 block storage container (one of each white, orange, blue)

Important Steps	Key Points	Reasons
A logical segment of the operation when something happens to advance the work	Anything in a step that might... 1. Make or break the job 2. Injure the worker 3. Make the work easier to do, i.e., "knack," "trick," special timing, bit of special information.	Reasons for the key points.
1. Observe Kanban Pad	Closely monitor each color Kanban Pad for activity	To quickly respond to customer demand as a Part is taken from inventory
2. Observe Removal of Product from Kanban Pad	Pay close attention to the color of the Part removed	To quickly start production of the correct color of product when it is in demand
3. Select Part B	Pick the correct color Part B based on the part removed from the Kanban Pad	Select the right materials the first time with no rework or errors
4. Select 2X2 block	Use the correct color block based on the part removed from Kanban Pad	Select the right materials the first time with no rework or errors
5. Secure 2X2 block to Part B	Connect the 2X2 to Part B so it forms one solid rectangular component	Build the right product the first time with no rework or errors
6. Place Final Product on Kanban Pad	Place the Final Product on the correct color Kanban Pad	Clearly communicate at a glance that the correct colored product is available

3.05 Review Project Charter with Kaizen Team

Overview

During the Review Project Charter activity the Kaizen Facilitator simply reviews the Kaizen Event project charter with the Kaizen Event team. The Kaizen Facilitator builds consensus around project and process scope by reviewing the problem statement and other components of the charter, discussing the pre-Kaizen Event deep dive results, and facilitating a general discussion about the process metrics and improve goals. The Kaizen Facilitator can update the Kaizen Event charter to reflect the current state of the process, metrics, or goals.

Objective

- Build consensus around the scope of the project and the process
- Clearly communication the operational definitions of the primary metric
- Understand the critical factors identified during the Pre-Kaizen deep dive
- Update the charter to represent the current state of the opportunity

Estimated Time to Complete

10 to 30 Minutes

Inputs (Resources required by the process)	Where/From
Kaizen Facilitator	You
Kaizen Event Team	Project Sponsor
Project Sponsor	Organization
Kaizen Event Project Charter	2.05 Draft Kaizen Charter Activity
Conference Room	Organization

Outputs (Deliverables from the process)	Possible Metrics
Consensus on Project and Process Scope	Number of Questions, Number of Parking lot items.

Steps to Complete

1. Handout current state Kaizen Event Project Charter

2. Review each element of the project charter

3. Review baseline performance data

4. Update the Kaizen Event project charter scope and process scope if necessary

Process Kaizen

4. Define Process

Overview

During the Define Process sub-process the Kaizen Facilitator reviews the SIPOC and Process Mapping approaches used in defining the current state of the process. The Kaizen Facilitator then facilitates an affinity diagramming session to brainstorm the high level process. The results of Affinity Diagramming are used to populate a high level process document (SIPOC), build consensus around the inputs, outputs, customers, and suppliers for the process, and identify all the supporting activities for each sub-process identified.

Objective

- Progressively elaborate the current state of the process
- Build consensus on the current state of the process
- Identify 3-7 sub-processes for the overall process
- Identify activities required to successfully complete the process

4.01 Review SIPOC Approach

Overview

During the Review SIPOC Approach activity, the Kaizen Facilitator distributes the Understanding SIPOC Document to the Project Team Member(s) and reviews the SIPOC acronym, the steps to complete the SIPOC, why a SIPOC is used, and an example SIPOC.

Objective

- Understand the importance of high-level process brainstorming
- Learn the steps to complete a SIPOC document

Estimated Time to Complete

5 to 15 Minutes

Inputs (Resources required by the process)	Where/From
Kaizen Facilitator	You
Project Team Member(s)	Project Sponsor; Process Owner
Understanding SIPOC Document	Figure 4.01.01
Conference Room	Organization

Outputs (Deliverables from the process)	Possible Metrics
Understanding of SIPOC activity	Time to Review; Number of Questions; Number of Parking Lot items

Steps to Complete

1. Handout Understanding SIPOC Document

2. Review SIPOC acronym

3. Review SIPOC steps to complete

4. Review "Why do we use a SIPOC?"

5. Review example SIPOC

Figure 4.01.01 – Understanding the SIPOC

Understanding the SIPOC

What is SIPOC (Pronounced *Sigh-Pock*)?

Identifying the basic elements of a process is the first step in understanding it. The SIPOC is a high level process map used by process improvement teams to identify all relevant suppliers, inputs, process, outputs, and customers of a process improvement project before work begins. The SIPOC helps establish the scope of the process and builds a common vision among team members.

Understanding the SIPOC Acronym	Definition
Supplier	A source of materials, service or information input provided to a process.
Inputs	The products, services and material obtained from suppliers to produce the outputs delivered to customers.
Process	A set of interrelated work activities characterized by a set of specific inputs and value added tasks that make up a procedure for a set of specific outputs.
Outputs	Products, materials, services or information provided to customers (internal or external), from a process.
Customer	Anyone who receives a deliverable from the process

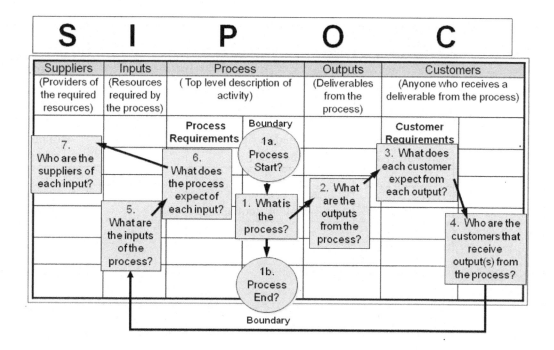

Why do we use a SIPOC?

- Establish the scope of the process (how the process starts and ends)
- Identify all the relevant elements of the process and build consensus around the process
- Define and communicate the true essence of the process to stakeholders
- Clear any doubts that might impede the process improvement effort
- Improve communication between all process team members

Figure 4.01.02 - Example SIPOC

Suppliers	Inputs	DMAIC Project Process	Outputs	Customers
Providers of the required resources	Resources required by the process	Top level description of the activity	Deliverables from the process	Anyone who receives a deliverable from the process
		Trigger: Continuous Improvement Request		
Process Owner Project Sponsor Continuous Improvement Company	Opportunity Communicated TAM Project Cluster List Process Owner Project Sponsor Continuous Improvement Project Charter Template Understanding DMAIC Document	1. Identify Opportunity	Continuous Improvement Discovery Meeting Process Identified Project Team Members Identified DMAIC Project Kick Off Meeting	Project Sponsor Process Owner Project Team Member(s) Kaizen Facilitator
Process Owner Project Sponsor Continuous Improvement Company	Process Identified Project Team Member(s) Process Owner DMAIC Project Kick Off Meeting Conference Room Computer Projector SIPOC Template Process Map Template	2. Define Process	Completed SIPOC Process Activities and Flow (Process Maps) Drafted Process Definition Document	Project Sponsor Process Owner Project Team Member(s) Kaizen Facilitator

	Kaizen Facilitator			
Process Owner Project Sponsor Continuous Improvement Company	Process Activities and Flow (Process Maps) Drafted Process Definition Document Project Team Member(s) Kaizen Facilitator Process Owner Value Added Flow Analysis Presentation Conference Room Computer Projector	3. Measure Process	Primary Metric(s) Identified Process Times and Lag Times Value Added Flow Analysis Completed Updated Process Definition Document (Activity Inputs and Outputs) Completed Current State Process Maps	Project Sponsor Process Owner Project Team Member(s) Kaizen Facilitator
Process Owner Project Sponsor Continuous Improvement Company	Project Team Member(s) Kaizen Facilitator Process Owner Updated Process Definition Document (Activity Inputs and Outputs) Cause and Effect Matrix Failure Modes Effect Analysis Template Conference	4. Analyze Process	Prioritized Inputs Prioritized Outputs Recommended Actions Analyze Phase Summary Graph Completed Cause and Effect Analysis Completed Failure Modes Effects Analysis	Project Sponsor Process Owner Project Team Member(s) Kaizen Facilitator

	Room Computer Projector			
Process Owner Project Sponsor Continuous Improvement Company	Recommended Actions Project Team Member(s) Kaizen Facilitator Process Owner Project Sponsor	5. Improve Process	Improvements Implemented Improve Phase Summary Presentation Updated Failure Modes Effects Analysis	Project Sponsor Process Owner Project Team Member(s) Kaizen Facilitator Process Stakeholder Seller

4.02 Develop SIPOC

Overview

During the Develop SIPOC activity the Kaizen Facilitator leads development of the SIPOC document through high-level process brainstorming to identify the suppliers, inputs, process, outputs, and customers of the process before detailed work begins. High level process brainstorming is facilitated using the Affinity Diagramming process, which allows large numbers of ideas to be sorted into groups for review and analysis and categorized into sub-processes.

Objective

- Empower individual think as well as group think
- Establish the scope of the process
- Improve communication between project team members
- Build consensus around the process

Estimated Time to Complete

45 to 60 Minutes

Inputs (Resources required by the process)	Where/From

Inputs (Resources required by the process)	Where/From
Understanding of SIPOC activity	Project Team Member
Project Team Member(s)	Organization
Kaizen Facilitator	You
SIPOC Template	Figure 4.02.01
Conference Room	Organization
Computer	Organization
Projector	Organization

Outputs (Deliverables from the process)	Possible Metrics
Completed SIPOC	Number of Sub-processes; Time to Complete; Number of Inputs; Number of Outputs, Number of Customers; Number of Suppliers

Steps to Complete

1. Establish process start trigger and end state

2. Project team members write down 3-7 activities or deliverables for the process on sticky notes (7 minutes)

3. Project Team Members stick ideas to wall

4. Project Team Members have 10 minutes to group the stickies into like areas or categories, without speaking a single word

5. Project Team Members define the categories as sub-processes

6. Establish 3-7 high-level process steps

7. Establish process end state

8. Define process step outputs

9. Define internal and external customers receiving outputs

10. Define inputs required to success complete process steps

11. Define internal and external providers of inputs

12. Save SIPOC to computer

13. Send communication Project Team Members with information and link

Figure 4.02.01 – SIPOC Template

Suppliers	Inputs	Process		Outputs	Customers	
(Providers of the required resources)	(Resources required by the process)	(Top level description of the activity)		(Deliverables from the process)	(Anyone who receives a deliverable from the process)	
		Requirements			Requirements	
			Trigger:			
			1.			
			2.			
			3.			
			4.			
			5.			

Process Kaizen

4.03 Review Process Map Approach

Overview

During the Review Process Map Approach activity the Kaizen Facilitator distributes the Understanding Process Maps document and reviews the Standard Process Design Model, common Business Process Design terminology, the steps to complete the Process Map, and the characteristics of a well defined process.

Objective

- Understand the importance of Process Mapping
- Learn the steps to develop a Process Map

Estimated Time to Complete

5 to 15 Minutes

Inputs (Resources required by the process)	Where/From
Project Team Member(s)	Project Sponsor; Process Owner
Kaizen Facilitator	You
Understanding Process Maps Document	Figure 4.03.01
Conference Room	Organization

Outputs (Deliverables from the process)	Possible Metrics
Understanding of Process Mapping Activity	Time to Review; Number of Questions; Number of Parking Lot items

Steps to Complete

1. Handout Understanding Process Maps document

2. Review Standard Process Design Model

3. Review Common Terminology

4. Review Steps to Complete a Process Map

5. Review Characteristics of a well defined process

Figure 4.03.01 – Understanding Process Maps

Understanding Process Maps

What is a Process Design?

Business process design is the method by which an organization understands and defines the business activities that enable it to function. Process design is concerned with designing a business' processes to ensure that they are optimized, effective, meet customer requirements, supporting and sustaining organizational development and growth. A well-designed process will improve efficiency and deliver greater productivity.

Standard Process Design Model

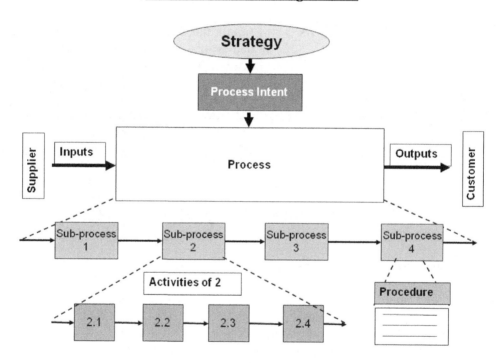

Understanding the Process Design Model	Description
Strategy	Strategy is the means by which the organization creates its unique and sustainable value toward fulfillment of the vision and objective. Strategy sets the general direction for the organization and is aligned to deliver the optimal flow of resources to achieve a

Understanding the Process Design Model	Description
	desired state in the future.
Process Intent	Process Intent is a description of the unique value a process delivers to customers.
Sub-processes	Sub-processes are logical subsets of organized steps and activities within the process that convert one or more input into one or more outputs. Sub-processes are directed toward a specific result or objective and can be considered key phases within a larger process.
Process Inputs and Outputs	Inputs and Outputs are the combined set of deliverables that a process utilizes to reach the desired process result as well as creates to deliver value and/or support another process.
Activities	Activities are the organized tasks and procedures for a sub-process.
Procedures	Procedures are the lowest level of detail in a process. Procedures can usually be accomplished by a single person and require very little coordination to finish.

Steps to complete a process map

1. Complete high level process map (SIPOC)
2. Detail 3-7 key sub-processes
3. Estimate process times and wait times
4. Define the inputs and outputs for each step
5. Identify all steps in the process as value added and non-value added
6. Identify 1-3 relevant measurement opportunities for each sub-process

Characteristics of a well designed process	
• Repeatable and reproducible • Consistent (Reduces re-work) • Effective and Efficient • Mitigates risk	• Can and should be measured • Can be drawn & communicated • Enables great adaptability for growth and change

Sub-process Map Example

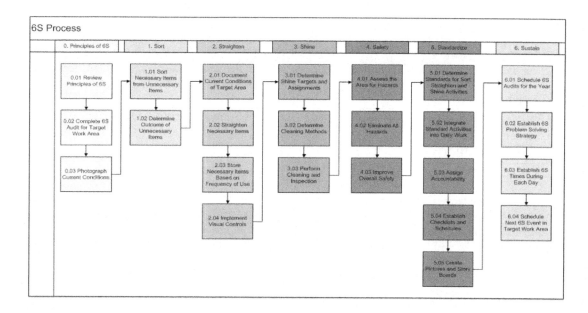

Why do we design processes?

- The need to increase efficiency
- The need to evaluate business practices as part of an organizational development project
- The need to evaluate potential new business ventures or business offerings
- The need to manage the company's knowledge resources
- The need to manage human resources

4.04 Define Level 1 Process Map

Overview

During the Define Level 1 Process Map activity the Kaizen Facilitator facilitates development of the high-level Process Map, including the sub-processes and flow of the key elements of the SIPOC. Project Team Members identify process start triggers and process end states in addition to the 3-7 key sub-processes.

Objective

- Define Process start and end states
- Define Sub-processes and Flow

Estimated Time to Complete

5 to 10 Minutes

Inputs (Resources required by the process)	Where/From
Understanding of Process Mapping Activity	Project Team Member
Project Team Member(s)	Project Sponsor; Process Owner
Kaizen Facilitator	You
Completed SIPOC	Project Team Members
Kaizen Event Process Map Template	Figure 4.04.01

Outputs (Deliverables from the process)	Possible Metrics
Level 1 Process Map	Time to Complete; Number of Sub-processes

Steps to Complete

1. Review SIPOC process steps

2. Open Process Map Template

3. Define Process Start Trigger Event

4. Populate Sub-processes from SIPOC

5. Define Process End State

Process Kaizen

Figure 4.04.01 – Process Map Template

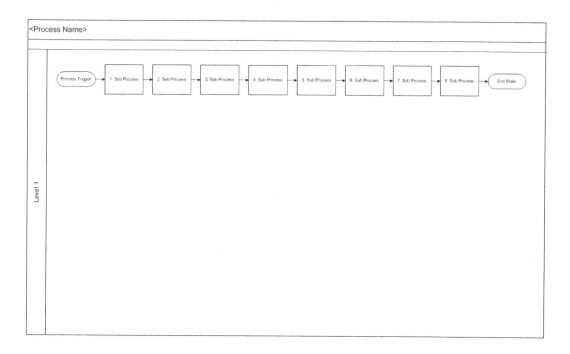

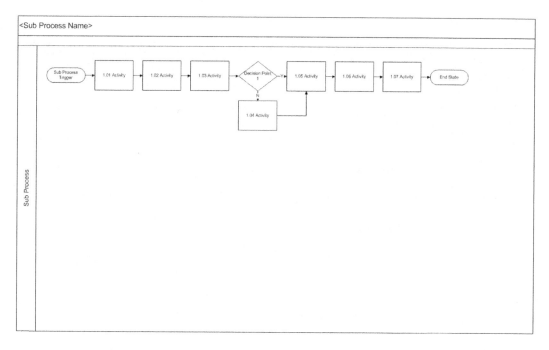

Figure 4.04.02 – Process Level 1 Process Map Example

4.05 Define Sub-process Maps

Overview

During the Define Sub-process Maps activity, the Kaizen Facilitator develops detailed Sub-process Maps. Project Team Members utilize the SIPOC to provide greater detail into the activities, decision points, and process flow for each Sub-process.

Objective

- Define Current State "As Is" Sub-process Activities and Flow
- Define Sub-process Decision Points

Estimated Time to Complete

90 to 150 Minutes

Inputs (Resources required by the process)	Where/From
Understanding of Process Mapping Activity	Project Team Members
Project Team Member(s)	Project Sponsor; Process Owner
Kaizen Facilitator	You
Completed SIPOC	Project Team Members
Process Map Template	Figure 1.04.01
Level 1 Process Map	4.04 Define Level 1 Process Maps

Outputs (Deliverables from the process)	Possible Metrics
Process Activities and Flow (Process Maps)	Time to Complete; Number of Sub-process Activities; Number of Decision Points

Steps to Complete

1. Develop Sub-process Map tabs

2. Define Sub-process Start Trigger Event

3. Define Sub-process Activities, Flow, and Decision Points

4. Define Sub-process End State

Figure 4.05.01 – Sub-process Map Example

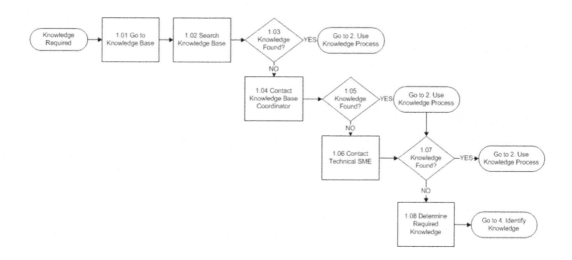

4.06 Finalize Define Phase Process Maps

Overview

During the Finalize Define Phase Process Maps activity, the Kaizen Facilitator cleans up the developed Process Map and ensures that Process Maps make sense and are complete. The Kaizen Facilitator is responsible for developing both PDF and HTML versions of the Process Maps and saving the Process Map file to a Networked Folder.

Objective

- Communicate Define phase process maps
- Prepare process maps for measurement and analysis

Estimated Time to Complete

15 to 30 Minutes

Inputs (Resources required by the process)	Where/From
Kaizen Facilitator	You
Process Activities and Flow (Process Maps)	Project Team Members
Process Map Standards	Process Kaizen – Figure 1.06.01

Outputs (Deliverables from the process)	Possible Metrics
Define Phase Process Maps	Time to Complete; Number of Updates
Folder Link	Time to Send

Steps to Complete

1. Review Level 1 Process Map

2. Integrate Sub-process Map Floating Activities and Decision Points

4. Convert Process Map to PDF

5. Convert Process Map to HTML

3. Save Versions of Process Map to network folder

6. Send communication to Project Team Member(s) with information and link

Figure 4.06.01 – Process Map Standards

The Purpose of Process Map Standards is to:

1. Convey a common understanding of the basis for documenting work processes by defining the five levels of detail for capturing work processes
2. Provide instructions for documenting work processes by indicating appropriate symbols and indicating ideas for modification to suit specific stakeholder needs
3. Provide guidelines for identifying work process Standard Work

Objectives

- Gather and document existing core business processes
- Understand the details and breakdown of the core business functions
- Identify issues and concerns with the core business functions and existing processes

- Allow the process owners to redesign, modify and adjust the existing processes based on their emerging requirements and internal drivers
- All the process owners to develop the controls and business process improvement steps to continuously improve business operations and make adjustments as required

What are the Five Levels of Detail for a Process?

1. Core Business Work Process
2. Key Function
3. Process
4. Activity
5. Standard Work and/or Standard Operating Procedures

Level 1 – Core Business Work Process

A core business work process is a collection of activities that accept inputs, act upon the inputs, and create output that is valuable to the organizations internal or external customers. Core business work processes are fundamental to the organization. There will usually be between 10 and 20 core business work processes that serve both external and internal customers. Some examples of core business work processes include forecasting, purchasing, distribution, HR, Finance, Support, etc.

Level 2 – Key Function

A key function is the first level of a core business work process. We often call these Level 1 or High Level Process Maps. There are typically 3 to 7 key functions to a core business work process. Each function includes activities that contribute to completing the core business work process. For example,

Level 3 –Process

Processes are comprised of sub-processes which are in turn comprised of a series, or flow, of activities that accomplish a single purpose, contributing to the completion of the key function of a core process.

Level 4 – Activities

Activities are the first level decomposition of processes. Activities traditionally complete a single deliverable required to meet a process objective. A process or sub-process are comprised of one or more activities. Activities generally start or finish when an objective or result changes, work is handed off to someone, or there is a break in the contiguous time it takes to complete the process deliverables.

Level 5 – Standard Work and/or Standard Operating Procedures

Standard Work is the lowest level of instructions for a particular activity and can usually be performed by a single person and usually employ a single form of technology. Each step in Standard Work must occur in the same contiguous time period and all appropriate steps must be completed to produce a meaningful deliverable.

During Kaizen Events, Project Teams should diagram the process at the level that exposes the issues. Issues at the activity and Standard Work level are excellent areas to be addressed during implementation. In fact, it is often recommended that during implementation the team completely redesign each activity and Standard Work to ensure that Standard Work supports the vision established during the Kaizen Event.

4.07 Draft Process Definition Document

Overview

During the Draft Process Definition Document activity, the Kaizen Facilitator develops the beginning of the Process Definition Document by inserting the Level 1 and Sub-process Maps and copying the framework for documenting process activities for each sub-process and activity.

Objective

- Prepare for Identification of Process Inputs and Outputs
- Develop a standard method for process and procedure documentation

Estimated Time to Complete

30 to 60 Minutes

Inputs (Resources required by the process)	Where/From
Process Definition Document Template	Process Kaizen – Figure 4.07.01
Kaizen Facilitator	You
Define Phase Process Maps	4.06 Finalize Define Phase Process Maps Activity

Outputs (Deliverables from the process)	Possible Metrics
Drafted Process Definition Document	Time to Complete
Deliverable Link	Time to Send

Steps to Complete

Process Kaizen

1. Copy Level 1 Process Map and Sub-processes to Word document

2. Copy Standard Process Definition format for each activity

3. Update Activity title for each Sub-process Activity

4. Save Process Definition Document to a network folder

5. Save Process Definition Document as HTML

6. Send communication to Project Team Member(s) with information and link

Figure 4.07.01 – Process Definition Document Template

<Insert Level 1 Process Map>

<Insert Sub-process Map 1>

1.01 Sub-process Activity

Overview

The Overview section is a narrative description of the activity. The Overview section describes how process inputs are used to deliver process outputs and is focused on the roles completing each step in the activity.

Objective

- Objectives are bulleted goals and expected results

Estimated Time to Complete

Time estimated to complete in minutes

Inputs (Resources required by the process)	Where/From

Outputs (Deliverables from the process)	Possible Metrics

Steps to Complete

The Steps to Complete section is used to provide the step by step sequence of events required to successfully complete the activity.

<Copy Activity section for the number of activities in sub-process>

<Copy Sub-process Map 2, etc.>

Figure 4.07.01 – Process Definition Document Example

Process Kaizen Book is in the format of a Process Definition Document.

5. Measure Process

Overview

During the Measure Process, the Project Team estimates process times and lag times, identifies and collects primary metrics data, identifies value added vs. non value added activities and defines the inputs and outputs necessary to complete each identified activity. The Kaizen Facilitator updates the process maps with the new information and finalized the current state process maps. The Kaizen Facilitator also creates the beginning of a Process Definition Document in order to document the activity inputs and outputs.

Objective

- Estimate or calculate process times and lag times
- Understand the concept of Value Added activities
- Identify Value Added and Non Value Added activities
- Identify required resources and expected outputs for each activity

5.01 Establish Level 1 Process Times and Lag Times

Overview

During the Establish Level 1 process Times and Lag Times activity the Kaizen Facilitator populates high-level process times and wait times. Project Team Members utilize the SIPOC and Level 1 Process Map to estimate the time it takes to complete each sub-process and the possible amount of time that might pass between each sub-process step.

Objective

- Develop high-level estimate for how long the process takes
- Estimate how much time is spent waiting during the process
- Estimate how long each sub-process takes

Estimated Time to Complete

15 to 30 Minutes

Inputs (Resources required by the process)	Where/From
Project Team Member(s)	Organization
Kaizen Facilitator	You
Define Phase Process Maps	4.06 Finalize Define Phase Process Maps
Conference Room	Organization
Computer	You
Projector	Organization
Process Map Standards	Figure 4.06.01
Completed SIPOC	4.02 Complete SIPOC Activity

Outputs (Deliverables from the process)	Possible Metrics
Level 1 Process Times and Lag Times	Total Process Time, Total Lag Time; Ratio of Process Time to Lag Time

Steps to Complete

1. Estimate Level 1 Sub-process Time

2. Estimate Level 1 Sub-process Lag Time

3. Summarize Level 1 Process Time

4. Summarize Level 1 Process Lag Time

5.02 Determine Level 1 Primary Metric(s)

Overview

During the Determine Level 1 Primary Metric(s) activity, the Kaizen Facilitator assists Project Team Members in identifying 1-3 key measurements that communicate process success and failure.

Objective

- Identify key factors for success in the process
- Identify measures for outputs

Estimated Time to Complete

5 to 15 Minutes

Inputs (Resources required by the process)	Where/From
Project Team Member(s)	Organization
Kaizen Facilitator	You
Define Phase Process Maps	4.06 Finalize Define Phase Process Maps
Conference Room	Organization
Computer	You
Projector	Organization
Process Map Standards	Figure 4.06.01

Outputs (Deliverables from the process)	Possible Metrics
Level 1 Process Primary Metric(s)	Number of Primary Metrics; Data Type; Metric Type; Data Collection Plan

Steps to Complete

1. Identify 1-3 measurement opportunities for process success

5.03 Estimate Sub-process Times and Lag Times

Overview

During the Estimate Sub-process Times and Lag Times activity, Project Team Members estimate the times for each activity in all sub-processes. After the team estimates process times, the Kaizen Facilitator facilitates estimation of wait times between each activity.

Objective

- Determine time range for activity times
- Document traditional lag times between activities

Estimated Time to Complete

30 to 90 Minutes

Inputs (Resources required by the process)	Where/From
Project Team Member(s)	Organization
Kaizen Facilitator	You
Define Phase Process Maps	4.06 Finalize Define Phase Process Maps
Conference Room	Organization
Computer	You
Projector	Organization
Process Map Standards	Figure 4.06.01

Outputs (Deliverables from the process)	Possible Metrics
Sub-process Times and Lag Times	Total Sub-process Time; Total Sub-process Lag Time; Ration of Sub-process Time to Sub-process Lag Time;

Steps to Complete

1. Estimate Sub-process Activity Times

2. Estimate Sub-process Activity Lag Time

3. Summarize Sub-process Time

4. Summarize Sub-process Lag Time

5.04 Determine Sub-process Primary Metric(s)

Overview

During the Determine Sub-process Primary Metric(s) activity, the Kaizen Facilitator assists Project Team Members in identifying 1-3 key measurements that communicate sub-process success and failure.

Objective

- Identify key factors for success in each sub-process
- Identify measures for outputs for each sub-process

Estimated Time to Complete

30 to 60 Minutes

Inputs (Resources required by the process)	Where/From
Project Team Member(s)	Organization
Kaizen Facilitator	You
Define Phase Process Maps	4.06 Finalize Define Phase Process Maps
Conference Room	Organization
Computer	You
Projector	Organization
Process Map Standards	Figure 4.06.01

Outputs (Deliverables from the process)	Possible Metrics
Sub-process Primary Metric(s)	Number of Primary Metrics; Data Type; Metric Type; Data Collection Plan

Steps to Complete

1. Identify 1-3 measurement opportunities for Sub-process success

5.05 Review Value Added Flow Analysis Approach

Overview

During the Review Value Added Flow Analysis Approach, the Kaizen Facilitator facilitates a presentation covering the definition of value added activities, the approach and goal of Value Added Flow Analysis, and the eight common wastes found in all business processes.

Process Kaizen

Project Team Members also discuss Value Added Flow Analysis and its benefits before completing Value Added Flow Analysis on their process.

Objective

- Understand Value Added Flow Analysis
- Ability to Apply Value Added Flow Analysis to any process
- Understand the 8 common wastes found in all processes

Estimated Time to Complete

25 Minutes

Inputs (Resources required by the process)	Where/From
Project Team Member(s)	Organization
Kaizen Facilitator	You
Understanding Value Added Flow Analysis Handout	Figure 5.05.01
Conference Room	Organization
Computer	You
Projector	Organization

Outputs (Deliverables from the process)	Possible Metrics
Understanding of Value Added Flow Analysis Approach	Number of Parking Lot Items; Number of Team Members Trained

Steps to Complete

1. Review Understanding Value Added Flow Analysis Handout

2. Summarize principles and definitions for Value Added Flow Analysis activity

3. Facilitate Questions and Answers

Figure 5.05.01 Understanding Value Added Flow Analysis

Understanding Value Added Flow Analysis

Value is defined by the customer. The customer always determines what is important to him or her and what is required in order to do business with him or her. Certainly, customer satisfaction is a function of cost, quality and delivery of a product or service. But how can you stay focused on the customer and determine what they value? This is especially true when price is matched by competition.

For something to add value:

1. The customer must be aware of it and care about it
2. It must change the product or service
3. It must be done right the first time
4. It must meet the customer's needs or specifications
5. It must be something the customer is willing to pay for

Something is non value added if:

1. The customer is unwilling to pay for it
2. Introduces time, resources, cost, or space but no value

Non value added activities traditionally fall into the 8 deadly wastes identified by Taiichi Ohno in 1922.

8 Deadly Wastes	
[Wheel diagram with segments: Processing, Transportation, Defects, Overproduction, Intellect, Motion, Waiting, Inventory, centered on WASTE]	**Defects** – Failings or flaws that may allow the affected thing to function, however imperfectly **Overproduction** – Production of something in excess of what is required by the **customer** **Waiting** – A period of time delay spent while expecting something to happen or ready for something to happen **Transportation** – Excessive movement of people or things within the process **Inventory** – Stock that an organization has on hand beyond what is considered necessary **Motion** – Movement of people or parts that does not add value to the product or service **Extra Processing** – Effort that adds no value to the product or service from the

	customers' viewpoint
	Intellect/Under-Utilized Talents – Peoples' abilities not effectively or appropriately used

Process mapping is the first step in understanding where the waste is within a process. By mapping the process, you create a visual baseline that becomes a key element in gaining group consensus of what the process is and where the opportunities exist. In many cases, this is your first real opportunity to understand the REAL process versus everyone's different versions of the process in their heads.

Examples of Waste in different industries and processes

Waste in Production Processes

- **Defects**: Incorrect processing, scrap, rework, incorrect quantities shipped

- **Overproduction**: Batching product to maximize machine efficiency

- **Transportation**: Extra walking or material movement in the process, no point of use materials, long process

- **Waiting**: Batch methods, machine waiting for man – Man waiting for machine

- **Inventory**: Built to stock rather than built to customer pull

- **Motion**: Extra steps, extra body motion, inefficient machine cycle/travel

- **Processing**: Extra processing of material, i.e., machining, cleaning

- **Intellect**: Not listening to employees' ideas who are involved first hand in the actual work

Waste in Business Administrative Processes

- **Defects:** Incorrect data entry

- **Over production:** Preparing extra reports, reports not acted upon, batch practices

- **Transportation:** Extra steps in the process, distance traveled

- **Waiting:** Batch methods, choppy workflow, i.e., closings, billings, collections

- **Inventory:** Transactions not processed, in- and out-baskets, signature cycle rooms

- **Motion:** Extra steps, extra data entry, information not at point-of-use

- **Processing:** Sign-offs and approvals

- **Intellect:** Not acting on employee complaints about legitimate problems and solutions

Waste in Design and Software Development Processes

- **Defects:** Miscommunication, drawing errors

- **Over production:** No standardization or reuse

- **Transportation:** Chasing approvals, data hand-offs

- **Waiting:** Approvals, Other Functions or Departments

- **Inventory:** Design data which is not organized or fully utilized, a quantity of designs in process that exceed capacity

- **Motion:** Unnecessary analysis, testing, or reviews

- **Processing:** Redesign, poorly run team meetings, sending or printing design files without request

- **Intellect:** Not incorporating front line workers in the process of new product design

5.06 Perform Value Added Flow Analysis

Overview

During the Perform Value Added Flow Analysis activity the Kaizen Facilitator facilitates the documentation of value added and non-value added activities in each sub-process. Project Team Members apply the strict definition of value added to determine whether each activity is important to the customer, changes the form or function of the product or service, and whether the activity is done right the first time.

Objective

- Determine the value added activities in each sub-process

- Determine the non-value added or business-value added activities in each sub-process
- Identify types of common waste in each sub-process

Estimated Time to Complete

15 to 30 Minutes

Inputs (Resources required by the process)	Where/From
Project Team Member(s)	Organization
Kaizen Facilitator	You
Define Phase Process Maps	4.06 Finalize Define Phase Process Maps
Conference Room	Organization
Computer	You
Projector	Organization
Understanding of Value Added Flow Analysis	Figure 5.06.01
Process Map Standards	Figure 4.06.01

Outputs (Deliverables from the process)	Possible Metrics
Completed Process Map	Number of Value Added Activities; Value Added Process Time; Number of Non Value Added Activities; Non-Value Added Process Time; Value Added Process Time to Non Value Added Process Time

Steps to Complete

1. Determine Value of each Sub-process Activity

5.07 Finalize Measure Phases Process Maps

Overview

During the Finalize Measure Phase Process Maps activity, the Kaizen Facilitator calculates process times and lag times in addition to value added times and non-value added times. The Kaizen Facilitator then publishes the Current State Process Map to a network folder and communicates the Published Current State Process Map to Project Team Members.

Objective

- Calculate Sub-process Times and Lag Times
- Calculate Sub-process Value Added Time and Non-Value Added Time
- Publish Current State Process Maps to a network folder
- Communicate Information and links to Project Team Members

Estimated Time to Complete

30 to 45 Minutes

Inputs (Resources required by the process)	Where/From
Kaizen Facilitator	You
Completed Process Map	5.06 Perform Value Added Flow Analysis

Outputs (Deliverables from the process)	Possible Metrics
Measure Phase Process Maps	Time to Complete; Number of Activities; Value Added vs. Non Value Added Process Times; Process Times and Lag Times
Current State Process Map Published on a network folder	Time to publish; Number of updates

Steps to Complete

1. Review Completed Process Map

2. Integrate Sub-process Map Floating Activities and Decision Points

3. Update/Save Process Map to a network folder

4. Update/Save Process Map to PDF

5. Update/Save Process Map to HTML

6. Send communication to Project Team Member(s) with information and link

5.08 Define Sub-process Activity Inputs and Outputs

Overview

During the Define Sub-process Activity Inputs and Outputs activity, the Kaizen Facilitator assists Project Team Members in identifying the inputs required to successfully complete each sub-process activity as well as the outputs generated by each activity. Inputs are the people, products, materials, services, tools, and information required to create the products, materials, and services provided to internal and external customers.

Objective

- Identify all sub-process inputs
- Identify all sub-process outputs

Estimated Time to Complete

90 to 120 Minutes

Inputs (Resources required by the process)	Where/From
Project Team Member(s)	Organization
Kaizen Facilitator	You
Measure Phase Process Maps	5.07 Finalize Measure Phase Process Maps
Conference Room	Organization
Computer	You
Projector	Organization
Drafted Process Definition Document	4.07 Draft Process Definition Document

Outputs (Deliverables from the process)	Possible Metrics
Process Inputs	Number of Inputs
Process Outputs	Number of Outputs
Updated Process Definition Document	Length of Document; Number of Activities; Number of Inputs and Outputs; Time to Publish

Steps to Complete

1. Identify resources required to successfully complete each Sub-process Activity

2. Identify the deliverables for each Sub-process Activity

6. Analyze Process

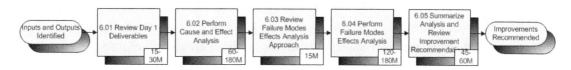

Overview

During the Analyze Process, the Kaizen Facilitator starts the second day of Kaizen by reviewing the deliverables created on Day 1. The Kaizen Facilitator then leads the team through Cause and Effect Analysis, followed by in depth Failure Modes Effect Analysis of the prioritized inputs of the process. The Project Team identified root causes to critical failure modes of the prioritized inputs and come up with recommended actions for reducing the occurrence of the causes or improving the organization's ability to detect and react to failures.

Objective

- Review and continue to build consensus on the current state process
- Analyze and prioritize the entire population of process inputs
- Further analyze the identified critical factors in the process
- Develop Lean solutions that eliminate root causes

6.01 Prepare Cause and Effect Matrix

Overview

During the Prepare Cause and Effect Matrix activity, the Kaizen Facilitator uses the Updated Process Definition Document with the identified sub-process activity inputs and outputs to prepare the Cause and Effect Matrix for analysis by Project Team Members. The Kaizen Facilitator eliminates any duplicate inputs and outputs and documents the list of inputs and outputs based on how and when they appear in the process.

Objective

- List process inputs
- List process outputs
- Populate Cause and Effect Matrix

Estimated Time to Complete

15 to 30 Minutes

Inputs (Resources required by the process)	Where/From
Kaizen Facilitator	You
Updated Process Definition Document	5.08 Define Sub-process Inputs and Outputs
Cause and Effect Matrix Template	Figure 6.01.01
Computer	You

Outputs (Deliverables from the process)	Possible Metrics
Prepared Cause and Effect Matrix	Number of Inputs; Number of Outputs; Time to Prepare

Steps to Complete

1. Review Updated Process Definition Document

2. Open Cause and Effect Matrix Template

3. List all Process Inputs

4. List all Process Outputs

5. Save Cause and Effect Matrix to a network folder

Figure 6.01.01 – Cause and Effect Matrix Template

Input #	Process Step	Rating of Importance to Customer										Total
			1	2	3	4	5	6	7	8	9	10	
			Output 1	Output 2	Output 3								
1		Input 1											0
2		Input 2											0
3		Input 3											0
													0
													0
													0
													0
													0
													0
													0
													0
													0
													0
													0
													0
													0
													0
													0
Total			0	0	0	0	0	0	0	0	0	0	

6.02 Perform Cause and Effect Analysis

Overview

During the Perform Cause and Effect Analysis activity, the Kaizen Facilitator provides a qualitative approach that quantifies the correlation of "How Important" certain inputs are relative to achieving goals, represented by process outputs. Project Team Members create a prioritized list of inputs and learn to apply the Pareto Principle, used to identify the top 20% of prioritized inputs for further analysis

Objective

- Analyze importance of process inputs
- Rank importance to customer of process outputs
- Calculate and sort input priorities
- Determine prioritized inputs for further analysis

Estimated Time to Complete

60 to 90 Minutes

Inputs (Resources required by the process)	Where/From
Project Team Member(s)	Organization
Kaizen Facilitator	You
Prepared Cause and Effect Matrix	6.01 Prepare Cause and Effect Matrix
Conference Room	Organization
Computer	You
Projector	Organization
Understanding Cause and Effect Analysis Handout	Figures 6.02.01 and 6.02.02

Outputs (Deliverables from the process)	Possible Metrics
Understanding of Cause and Effect Analysis	Number of Team Members Trained; Time to Review; Parking Lot Items
Completed Cause and Effect Matrix	Time to Complete; Prioritized list of Process Inputs

Steps to Complete

1. Review 0, 1, 4, 9 Ranking Scale as impact of an input on each output

2. Correlate Process Inputs to Outputs (Correlation Values)

3. Assign value to each Output using a 1-10 ranking scale (Output Values)

4. Cross-multiply Correlation Values with Output Values to calculate priority

5. Save updated Cause and Effect Analysis File to a network folder

6. Send communication to Project Team Member(s) with information and link

Figure 6.02.01 – Understanding Cause and Effect Analysis

Understanding Cause and Effect Analysis

The only way to manage and improve processes is by managing and improving the inputs going into those processes. But not all inputs are created equal. The Pareto principle suggests that 20% of a systems components (i.e., inputs) will influence 80% of that systems performance. But how do we know which of our various inputs are the most influential?

We use prioritization tools such as the Cause and Effect Matrix and the Failure Modes Effects Analysis to identify, explore and display the possible causes related to a problem or condition and probe to the level necessary to discover the root causes of the issues.

By starting with Cause and Effect analysis we are able to focus the team on the content of the problem by identifying the critical factors that influence the expected performance in the process. Cause and Effect analysis is a qualitative analysis activity that attempts to quantify the correlation of "how important" the inputs in the process are relative to achieving process outcome or goals, represented by certain outputs.

The activity is qualitative because we attempt to measure the effect or importance of inputs on outputs. This measurement is based first on subject matter expert opinion and validated with the use of data. The convergence of potential critical factors is based on a systematic progressive elaboration of Cause and Effect and Failure Modes Effects Analyses.

Your goal is to find the few, critical inputs that have the largest impact on the outputs.

Scoring Scales for Cause and Effect Analysis

We try to keep the correlation values for inputs and outputs as simple as possible, because the effort required to complete a Cause and Effect analysis can be significant. To avoid spending too much time in the assignment of scoring, use a simplified scoring criteria.

0 = No correlation

1 = The input only remotely or weakly influences the output

4 = The input moderately influences the output

9 = The input strongly and directly influences the output

You can rank the outputs on a scale of 1-10 and then use the value to find the critical factors.

Figure 6.02.02 – Cause and Effect Matrix Example

Rating of Importance to Customer	2	3	2	4	4	4	3	4	2	2	2	3	5	5	2	2	7	2	1	
	1	2	3	4	5	6	7	8	9	10	11	12	13	14	15	16	17	18	19	
Process Inputs / Process Input	Understanding of SIPOC activity	Completed SIPOC	Mapping Activity	Process Maps	Links	Process Definition Document	Process Times and Lag Times	Process Metrics	Flow Analysis Approach	Cause and Effect	Cause and Effect Analysis	Approach	Failure Modes Effect Analysis	Recommended Actions	FMEA Graph	Process Improvement Backlog	Implemented Improvements	Deliverables	Improvement Retrospective	Total
1 Kaizen Facilitator	9	9	9	9	9	9	9	9	9	9	9	9	9	9	9	9	4	4	9	486
2 Project Team Member(s)	9	9	9	9	1	9	9	9	9	9	9	9	9	9	1	9	9	9	9	483
3 Process Owner	9	9	9	9	1	4	9	9	9	9	9	9	9	9	1	9	9	9	4	458
4 Implemented Improvements	0	0	0	9	9	9	9	9	4	4	0	4	9	9	1	9	9	9	9	399
5 Process Definition Document	0	0	0	4	9	9	4	4	4	4	9	4	9	9	1	9	9	9	1	354
6 Completed Failure Modes Effects Analysis	0	0	0	9	9	9	0	0	0	0	0	9	9	9	9	9	9	9	1	343
7 Completed Process Map	0	0	0	9	9	9	0	0	0	0	9	9	9	9	9	4	4	9	4	319
8 Lean Tools	4	1	4	4	0	1	4	4	9	4	4	9	9	9	1	1	9	4	1	294
9 Process Map Standards	0	0	9	9	9	9	9	9	9	0	0	0	0	0	0	4	4	4	4	255
10 Sub-process Maps	0	0	9	9	9	9	9	9	4	0	0	0	0	0	0	4	4	4	1	242
11 Level 1 Process Map	0	0	9	9	9	9	9	9	0	0	0	0	0	0	0	0	0	0	0	189
12 Sprint Improvement Backlog	0	0	0	0	9	0	0	0	0	0	0	0	9	1	9	9	9	9	4	186
13 Computer	1	4	1	4	9	4	4	4	9	1	4	1	4	1	1	1	0	4	0	180
14 Cause and Effect Matrix Template	0	0	0	0	9	0	0	0	0	9	9	4	9	4	1	4	1	4	1	175
15 Cause and Effect Matrix	0	0	0	0	9	0	0	0	0	9	9	4	9	4	1	4	1	4	1	175
16 Project Sponsor	0	0	0	0	0	0	0	0	0	0	0	0	0	0	9	0	9	9	4	148
17 Process Map Template	0	0	9	9	9	4	4	4	0	0	0	0	0	0	0	1	1	1	1	146
18 Understanding of Process Mapping	0	0	4	9	0	4	9	9	1	0	0	0	0	0	0	4	1	1	1	143

Process Kaizen

Process Inputs		Rating of Importance to Customer	2	3	2	4	4	4	3	4	2	2	2	3	5	5	2	2	7	2	1	
			1	2	3	4	5	6	7	8	9	10	11	12	13	14	15	16	17	18	19	
	Process Input Activity		Understanding of SIPOC activity	Completed SIPOC	Mapping Activity	Process Maps	Links	Process Definition Document	Process Times and Lag Times	Process Metrics	Flow Analysis Approach	Cause and Effect	Cause and Effect Analysis	Approach	Failure Modes Effect Analysis	Recommended Actions	FMEA Graph	Process Improvement Backlog	Implemented Improvements	Deliverables	Improvement Retrospective	Total
19	Improvement Backlog Template		0	0	0	0	9	0	0	0	0	0	0	0	0	0	0	9	9	9	4	139
20	Conference Room		1	4	1	4	0	1	4	4	4	4	4	1	4	1	0	1	0	4	4	130
21	Understanding Process Maps Document		0	0	9	9	9	4	1	1	0	0	0	0	0	1	0	1	1	0	0	127
22	Failure Modes Effects Analysis Approach		0	0	0	0	9	0	0	0	0	0	0	9	9	1	1	1	1	1	1	127
23	Failure Modes Effects Analysis Template		0	0	0	0	9	0	0	0	0	0	0	9	9	1	1	1	1	1	1	127
Total			84	159	148	480	728	384	267	356	198	110	148	246	555	510	78	248	917	288	95	

6.03 Review Failure Modes Effect Analysis Approach

Overview

During the Review Failure Modes Effect Analysis Approach activity the Kaizen Facilitator reviews the structured approach to identifying ways in which a product or process can fail, estimating the risk associated with specific causes, and prioritizing the actions that should be taken to reduce the risk.

Objective

- Understand the steps to complete Failure Modes Effects Analysis
- Ability to apply Failure Modes Effects Analysis to any process
- Understand the importance of Failure Modes Effects Analysis

Estimated Time to Complete

15 Minutes

Process Kaizen

Inputs (Resources required by the process)	Where/From
Project Team Member(s)	Organization
Kaizen Facilitator	You
Conference Room	Organization
Computer	You
Projector	Organization
Understanding Failure Modes Effects Analysis Handout	Figure 6.03.01
Failure Modes Effects Analysis Template	Figure 6.03.02

Outputs (Deliverables from the process)	Possible Metrics
Understanding of Failure Modes Effects Analysis Approach	Number of Questions; Number of Parking Lot Items

Steps to Complete

1. Open Failure Modes Effects Analysis Template

2. Review Failure Modes Effects Analysis Format

3. Review Failure Modes Effects Analysis Example

Figure 6.03.01 – Understanding Failure Modes Effects Analysis

Understanding Failure Modes Effects Analysis

Failure Modes Effects Analysis is a structured approach to identifying ways in which a product or process can fail and uncovering the root causes to the failures. By taking the top 20% of process input variables and moving them into Failure Modes Effects Analysis, the project team can focus on eliminating or reducing the risk of failure in order to protect and delight the customer.

Understanding the FMEA Model	
Cause	The sources of process variation that causes the failure mode to occur. To identify all possible causes of failure modes continue to ask "Why?" the failure mode occurred. Examples of Effects include, oven temperature too high, doctor's prescription not legible, water treatment equipment failure, etc.
Failure Mode (Defect)	Failure modes are the ways in which a specific process input fails. Any scenario where the process input leads to negative effects on internal or external customers is considered a

Understanding the FMEA Model	
	failure mode. A negative effect is anything that is deemed unacceptable by a customer. Example of failure modes include burnt bread, incorrectly filled prescriptions, unsafe drinking water, etc.
Effect	Effects are the adverse impacts on customer requirements due to the product or process not performing satisfactorily based on the requirements of the customer. Examples include loss of sales, dangerous reactions to medicine, illness, etc.

The relationship between the failure mode and the effect is not always one to one. You can encounter a failure mode that leads to multiple effects or multiple failure modes leading to the same effect.

FMEA Rating Scales for Severity, Occurrence, and Detection			
Rating	**Severity**	**Occurrence**	**Detectability**
High (9-10)	Hazardous without warning	Very high and almost inevitable	Cannot detect or detection with very low probability
Medium High (7-8)	Loss of primary function	High repeated failures	Remote or low chance of detection
Medium (5-6)	Loss of secondary function	Moderate failures	Low detection probability
Medium Low(3-4)	Minor Defect	Occasional failures	Moderate Detection Probability
Low (1-2)	No effect	Failure Unlikely	Almost Certain Detection

Note: You should determine if your organization has rating scales and rules. In some organizations, a rating of "10" on severity may have legal consequences.

A key output of an FMEA is the "Risk Priority Number" or RPN. RPN is calculated based on the information provided in Severity, Occurrence, and Detectability. RPN represents the likelihood of potential causes of failure modes, the seriousness of the resulting effects and the organization's current ability to detect the causes or failure modes as they are occurring.

Regardless of RPN, high severity scores should be given special attention. Also, remember that a high detection score means that it is difficult to identify the causes or failure modes as they are occurring.

As you create and complete the FMEA, utilize the process maps, Cause and Effect analysis, data collection, subject matter experts, and other sources of information. It is also important to note that for any give process step or input, there can be more than one failure mode. And, for any give failure mode, there can be more than one potential cause. It is recommended to capture as many failure modes and possible causes as possible on the FMEA.

Figure 6.03.02 – Failure Modes Effects Analysis Template

Process Step	Key Process Input	Potential Failure Mode	Potential Failure Effects	SEV	Potential Causes	OCC	Current Controls	DET	RPN	EOC	Actions Recommended	Resp.	Actions Taken	SEV	OCC	DET	RPN
What is the process step	What is the Key Process Input?	In what ways does the Key Input go wrong?	What is the impact on the Key Output Variables (Customer Requirements) or internal requirements?	How Severe is the effect to the customer?	What causes the Key Input to go wrong?	How often does cause or FM occur?	What are the existing controls and procedures (inspection and test) that prevent either the cause or the Failure Mode? **Should include an SOP number.**	How well can you detect cause or FM?			What are the actions for reducing the occurrence of the Cause, or improving detection? **Should have actions only on high RPN's or easy fixes.**	Whose Responsible for the recommended action?	What are the completed actions taken with the recalculated RPN? **Be sure to include completion month/year**				

Figure 6.03.03 – Failure Modes Effects Analysis Example

Key Process Input	Potential Failure Mode	Potential Failure Effects	SEV	Potential Causes	OCC	Current Controls	DET	RPN	EOC	Actions Recommended
What is the Key Process Input?	In what ways does the Key Input go wrong?	What is the impact on the Key Output Variables (Customer Requirements) or internal requirements?	How Severe is the effect to the customer?	What causes the Key Input to go wrong?	How often does cause or FM occur?	What are the existing controls and procedures (inspection and test) that prevent either the cause or the Failure Mode? **Should include an SOP number.**	How well can you detect cause or FM?			What are the actions for reducing the occurrence of the Cause, or improving detection? **Should have actions only on high RPN's or easy fixes.**
Implemented Improvements	Recommended actions do not get completed in a timely fashion. Recommended actions do not get completed at all. Improvements are only partially completed. Improvements are not fully documented. Improvements are not communicated and trained.	Loss of process capability. Loss of efficiencies. Lost of financial benefits. Delay. Loss of trust in Continuous Improvement. Confusion. Loss of momentum.	8	Not enough time spent focusing on improvement tasks. Lack of understanding on how to create improvement deliverable. Shifting priorities. Lack of sense of urgency and commitment. No time planned and scheduled for Continuous Improvement activities. Too many FMEA recommended actions to deliver in a timely fashion.	8	Biweekly review of FMEA with Project Team and Process Owner where updates are made to Actions Taken cell as well as possible recalculation of RPN. Also have a Improvement Sprint project management model for teams that need assistance with planning and improvement implementation.	7	448	4	Develop a reaction plan for key failure modes during improvement implementation in order to control key factors during improve phase. Clearly communicate resource needs for implementing improvement and work with Process Owner and Project Sponsor to clearly communicate expectations to project team members. Identify process documentation and lean tools that can be immediately used by project team members.

6.04 Perform Failure Modes Effects Analysis

Overview

During the Perform Failure Modes Effects Analysis activity the Kaizen Facilitator facilitates analysis with Project Team Members through the use of the Failure Modes and Effects Analysis spreadsheet. Project Team Members identify ways that the process input can fail, how failure impacts what is delivered to the customer, what causes the input to fail, current controls and procedures, and what should be done to fix the input for the last time. The Kaizen Facilitator publishes the Failure Modes Effects Analysis spreadsheet to a network folder once the team has completed the activity.

Objective

- Identify ways that prioritized process inputs can fail
- Identify methods to eliminate or reduce the risk of failure in order to protect the customer
- Develop recommended actions for process improvement

Estimated Time to Complete

120 to 180 Minutes

Inputs (Resources required by the process)	Where/From
Project Team Member(s)	Organization
Kaizen Facilitator	You
Conference Room	Organization
Computer	You
Projector	Organization
Understanding of Failure Modes Effects Analysis Handout	Figure 6.03.01
Failure Modes Effects Analysis Template	Figure 6.03.02

Outputs (Deliverables from the process)	Possible Metrics
Process Input Risk Priority Number	Riskiness of Each Prioritized Input
Recommended Actions	Number of Recommended Actions; Number of Recommended Action that the Kaizen Event Team can manage
Completed Failure Modes Effects Analysis	Time to Complete; Time to Publish

Steps to Complete

1. Populate Prioritized List of Inputs (Top 20%)

2. Determine what can go wrong with the process input

3. Determine the effect on the Process Outputs when the input goes wrong

4. Determine the seriousness of the effect

5. Determine the causes of the failures

6. Determine how often the cause is likely to occur and result in a failure

7. Define what is currently being done to either prevent the causes or failures from occurring

8. Determine how well we detect a cause before it creates a failure or effect

9. Determine the actions for reducing the occurrence of the cause or improving detection

10. Identify a point of contact for the recommended actions

11. Estimate the ease of completion for the recommended actions

12. Save Failure Modes Effects Analysis file to a network folder

13. Send communication to Project Team Member(s) with information and link

6.05 Summarize Analysis and Review Improvement Recommendations

Overview

During the Summarize Analysis and Review Improvement Recommendations activity the Kaizen Facilitator finalizes the Failure Modes and Effects Analysis by calculating and sorting inputs Risk Priority Number and Ease of Completion. The Kaizen Facilitator develops Failure Modes Effects Analysis Graph and Project Summary Presentation, which is saved to the network Project Folder and communicated to Project Team Members.

Objective

- Summarize Recommended Actions for Process Improvement
- Communicate Process Deliverables to Project Team Members

Estimated Time to Complete

45 to 60 Minutes

Inputs (Resources required by the process)	Where/From
Kaizen Facilitator	You
Completed Failure Modes Effects Analysis	6.04 Perform Failure Modes Effects Analysis
Failure Modes Effects Analysis Graph Template	Process Kaizen – Figure 6.04.01
Analyze Phase Summary Presentation	Process Kaizen – Figure 6.04.01

Inputs (Resources required by the process)	Where/From
Template	

Outputs (Deliverables from the process)	Possible Metrics
Analyze Phase Summary Presentation	Time to Complete; Time to Publish
Failure Modes Effects Analysis Graph	Time to Complete

Steps to Complete

1. Develop Failure Modes Effects Analysis Summary, including critical factors and recommended actions to be implemented

2. Develop Analyze Phase Summary Presentation

3. Save Analyze Phase Summary Presentation to a network folder

4. Send communication to Project Team Member(s) with information and link

7. Improve Process

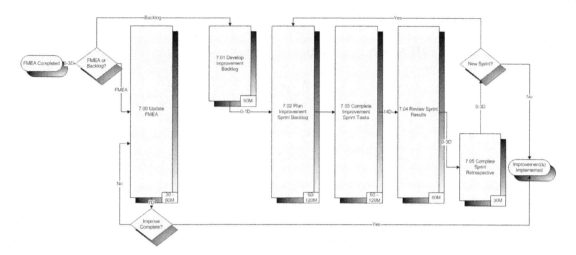

Overview

During the Improve Process the Kaizen Facilitator, Project Team, Process Owner and/or Project Sponsor review the recommended actions from the FMEA and determine the improvements that the team is capable of completing during the available hours for improvement activities. The Project Team reviews each selected recommended action and develops a Kaizen Improvement Backlog. The Project Team then implements the developed improvement plan over the next 2-3 days.

Objective

- Identify solutions that the team can implement
- Work on the riskiest items that are the easiest to complete
- Secure commitment to completing the work

7.01 Update FMEA

Overview

During the Update FMEA activity the Kaizen Facilitator reviews the recommended actions for process improvement and updates the document with any actions taken. Project Team Members also determine whether risk as been mitigated or eliminated and recalculate Risk Priority Numbers when appropriate. Project Team Members are responsible for interpreting the Failure Modes Effect Analysis and implementing improvements. This activity is taken when Project Team Members desire to manage improvements on their own and occurs every two weeks until improvements have been implemented.

Objective

- Review and document implemented improvements
- Resolve process improvement issues
- Review Project Team progress

Estimated Time to Complete

30 to 60 Minutes

Inputs (Resources required by the process)	Where/From
Failure Modes and Effects Analysis File	6.04 Perform Failure Modes Effects Analysis
Kaizen Facilitator	You
Project Team Member(s)	Organization
Process Owner	Organization
Project Sponsor	Organization

Outputs (Deliverables from the process)	Possible Metrics
Updated Failure Modes Effects Analysis File	Number of Updates; Time to Complete
Implemented Improvements	Number of Improvements Implemented; Change to Risk Priority Number; Number of Updates

Steps to Complete

1. Open Current Failure Modes Effect Analysis spreadsheet

2. Review each recommended action for improvement of process inputs

3. Document any actions taken based on recommended actions

4. Recalculate Input Risk Priority Numbers when risk has been mitigated or eliminated

7.02 Develop Improvement Backlog

Overview

During the Develop Improvement Backlog activity the Kaizen Facilitator works with the Process Owner and/or Project Sponsor to review the recommended actions in the Failure Modes Effect Analysis spreadsheet and begins identifying actionable items that can be accomplished within a two week sprint of improvement work. The Kaizen Facilitator also helps the Project Sponsor/Process Owner in calculating the available project team member hours for a sprint of two week improvement activities.

Objective

- Review and fully understand the Failure Modes Effect Analysis spreadsheet
- Identify actionable items
- Populate Improvement Backlog
- Describe the improvement item and done criteria
- Rank business reward and penalty

Estimated Time to Complete

60 Minutes

Inputs (Resources required by the process)	Where/From
Failure Modes and Effects Analysis	6.04 Perform FMEA
Kaizen Facilitator	You
Project Sponsor	Organization
Process Owner	Organization
Understanding Improvement Backlogs Handout	Figure 7.02.01
Improvement Backlog Template	Figure 7.02.02

Outputs (Deliverables from the process)	Possible Metrics
Process Improvement Backlog	Number of Backlog Items; Estimated Team Availability; Number of Tasks

Steps to Complete

1. Open Current Failure Modes Effect Analysis spreadsheet

2. Review each recommended action for improvement of process inputs

3. Identify Improvement Backlog Item(s)

4. Document Improvement Backlog Item(s) Name, Description, Reward, and Penalty

Figure 7.02.01 – Understanding Kaizen Event Improvement Backlogs

Understanding Kaizen Event Improvement Backlogs

Improvement Backlogs is a set of recommended actions coming from the Failure Modes Effects Analysis selected for the three improvement days of the Kaizen Event. Improvement Backlogs are progressively elaborated to include a plan for delivering the improvements and realizing the Kaizen Event goal. The Improvement Backlog is a forecast by the Kaizen Event Team about what improvements will be delivered and the work needed to deliver those improvements.

Ultimately, the Improvement Backlog puts the Kaizen Event Team in charge of their own improvement process and allows for rapid improvement within the process based on what the team can change and control.

It is important to keep the Improvement Backlog organized and prioritized for the Kaizen Event Team. The Improvement Backlog should only have the work that the team will be completing during the three days of the Kaizen Event improvement phase. If issues come up during improvement they should be documented as impediment and should be eliminated if possible.

Use the Improvement Backlog as the master list of all improvements desired during the Kaizen Event. The Improvement Backlog should be comprised of multiple backlog item. Each backlog item is first detailed by title, description, reward and penalty. These items are reviewed by the Kaizen Event Team and then improvement complexity, specific tasks, and task owners are defined.

Understanding the FMEA Model	
Backlog Item Title	The Backlog Item Title is the summary of a particular recommended action coming from the Failure Modes Effects Analysis (FMEA)
Backlog Item Description	The Backlog Item Description is comprised of two critical components – Stakeholder Story and Done Criteria. **Stakeholder Story** provides concise statement of

	Understanding the FMEA Model
	the desired improvement from the process stakeholder perspective. This is always documented "As an X, I need Y, so that I can Z." Example: As a chef, I need an oven with consistent temperature so that I can bake. **Done Criteria** provides a bulleted list of deliverables based on the Stakeholder Story. This is always documented "This is done when:" and a list of bulleted deliverables are identified.
Business Reward	Use the value of business reward (scale of 1-10) to determine the impact of implementing the improvement.
Business Penalty	Use the value of business penalty (scale of 1-10) to determine the impacts of not implementing the improvement. Remember, as a component of risk management there is always the option to do nothing- how much risk to we introduce into the process if we do nothing?
Improvement Complexity	Improvement Complexity is determined based on the complexity of the tasks required to successfully deliver the improvement, not how long it will take to implement the improvement. Complexity is scored based on the Fibonacci sequence of numbers to easily represent the scaling of complexity. Teams are asked to score Improvement Backlog Items based on the Backlog Item Description. The Team can ask questions to clarify the Backlog Item prior to committing to Improvement Complexity. The value progress as follows" 1 2 3 5 8 13 21 34 55. When a single improvement backlog item has a complexity of 34 or more, it may be too complex to complete during the Kaizen Event.
Improvement Tasks	Kaizen Event Team Members develop all of the tasks required to successfully deliver the improvement backlog item during the Kaizen Event. "Verb + Noun" tasks are identified, effort (not duration) is estimated, and a point of contact is identified.

It's important that you update the Improvement Backlog as tasks are completed and the Kaizen Event Team should review the tasks completed during the daily sprint meeting and identify and communicate impediments to completing their assigned tasks.

Once work starts, no new items should be added to the Improvement Backlog. The Improvement Backlog should represent the top priority items to complete during the 3 day sprint. This will help you keep scope creep down and increase the probability of completing all of the identified tasks.

Assist the Project Team when they encounter impediments that prevent them from completing their tasks and always leverage the Process Owner or Project Sponsor when necessary.

Figure 7.02.02 – Kaizen Event Improvement Backlog Template

Kaizen Event Improvement Backlog Item			
Backlog Item Title:			
<One sentence description of the improvement>			
Backlog Item Description:			
<As an X, I need Y, so that I can Z> This is done when: • Bulleted done criteria 1 • Bulleted done criteria 2			
Business reward when completed: (1 – 10 scale)			
Business penalty if not completed: (1 – 10 scale)			
Project Team Estimated Complexity: (Fibonacci Number) 1 2 3 5 8 13 21 34 55			
Task Description	Estimate in Minutes	Point of Contact	Minutes Burndown
		Total	

Process Kaizen

Figure 7.02.03 – Kaizen Event Improvement Backlog Example

Backlog Item Title:
Establish a baseline for requirements and contact information for all states and create a simple contact list
Backlog Item Description:
As a project team member I need an up-to-date list of all state points of contact that we currently work with so that I can effectively monitor and manage each states unique requirements. This is done when: • All current states identified • A contact is defined • The contact is contacted and verified • A list is published to the team • A schedule or responsibilities is developed to verify and update contact information • A determination where state documentation should be included in the list.
Business reward when completed: (1 – 10 scale)
5
Business penalty if not completed: (1 – 10 scale)
8
Project Team Estimated Complexity: (Fibonacci Number) 1 2 3 5 8 13 21 34 55
2

Task Description	Estimate in Minutes	Point of Contact	Minutes Burndown
		Total	

7.03 Plan Improvement Sprint Backlog

Overview

During the Plan Improvement Sprint Backlog activity the Kaizen Facilitator reviews the Improvement Backlog with Project Team Members. Project Team Members estimate improvement item complexity based on the done criteria description of the improvement item. Project Team Members also identify tasks and estimate the effort required to complete the improvement.

Objective

- Understand the proposed Improvement Backlog
- Understand done criteria for each Improvement Backlog Item
- Estimate Complexity of Improvement Backlog Item
- Identify and Estimate Tasks Required to Complete Improvement Backlog Item

Estimated Time to Complete

60 to 120 Minutes

Inputs (Resources required by the process)	Where/From
Process Improvement Backlog	7.02 Develop Improvement Backlog
Kaizen Facilitator	You
Process Owner	Organization
Project Sponsor	Organization
Project Team Member	Organization
Improvement Sprint Hours	Kaizen Event Project Team
Failure Modes Effect Analysis	6.04 Perform Failure Modes Effects Analysis
Process Definition Document	5.08 Define Sub-process Inputs and Outputs

Outputs (Deliverables from the process)	Possible Metrics
Improvement Tasks	Number of Tasks; Time per Task; Assigned Project Team Member
Task Commitments	Assigned Project Team Member
Improvement Sprint Hours Availability	Total Improvement Time
Improvement Sprint Backlog	Total Estimated Improvement Tasks

Steps to Complete

1. Review Process Improvement Backlog Name and Description

2. Estimate Process Improvement Backlog Item Complexity

3. Identify Tasks Required to Complete Process Improvement Backlog Item

4. Estimate Process Improvement Task Effort in Hours

Figure 7.03.01 – Understanding Improvement Planning

The Kaizen Facilitator is responsible for ensuring that everyone related to a Kaizen Event, whether kibitzers or Team members, follows the format of the Kaizen Event Improvement delivery process. These rules hold the Kaizen Event improvement process together so that everyone knows how to implement improvements. If the rules aren't enforced, people waste time figuring out what to do. If the rules are disputed, time is lost while everyone waits for a resolution. These rules have worked in literally thousands of successful projects. If someone wants to change the rules, use the Improvement Sprint Retrospective meeting as a forum for discussion. Rule changes should originate from the Team, not management. Rule changes should be entertained if and only if the Kaizen Facilitator is convinced that the Team and everyone involved understands how the Kaizen Event Improvement Delivery Process works in enough depth that they will be skillful and mindful in changing the rules. No rules can be changed until the Kaizen Facilitator has determined that this state has been reached.

Improvement Planning Meeting

The Improvement Planning Meeting is time-boxed to 2 hours and consists of two segments that are time-boxed to 1 hour each. The first segment is for selecting improvement backlog items; the second segment is for preparing the Improvement Sprint Backlog.

- Attendees are the Kaizen Facilitator, Team Members, Project Sponsor and/or the Process Owner. Additional parties can be invited by any of these people to provide additional business domain or industry domain information and advice, but they are dismissed after this information is provided. No kibitzers are allowed as observers of Phase 1 Planning.
- The Process Owner must prepare the Improvement Backlog prior to the meeting. In the absence of either the Process Owner or the Improvement Backlog, the Kaizen Facilitator is required to construct an adequate Improvement Backlog that maps a look ahead of possible improvement work based on Failure Modes and Effect Analysis recommended actions and to stand in for the Process Owner.
- The goal of the Phase 1 Planning, or the first 1 hour, is for the Team to select those Improvement Backlog items that it believes it can commit to turning into an implemented and fully documented improvement. The Team will demonstrate this functionality to the Process Owner and stakeholders at the Improvement Sprint Review meeting at the end of the Improvement Sprint.

- The Team can make suggestions, but the decision of what Improvement Backlog can constitute the Improvement Sprint is the responsibility of the Process Owner.
- The Team is responsible for determining how much of the Improvement Backlog that the Process Owner wants worked on the Team will attempt to do during the Improvement Sprint.
- Time-boxing the first segment to 1 hour means that this is all of the time that is available for analyzing the Improvement Backlog. Further analysis must be performed during the Improvement Sprint. Large-grained, high-priority Improvement Backlog with imprecise estimates might not be thoroughly understood during this part of the Improvement Sprint planning meeting and might result in the Team not being able to complete all of the Improvement Backlog that it selects.
- The second segment of the Sprint Planning meeting (Phase 2) occurs immediately after the first segment and is also time-boxed to 1 hour.
- The Process Owner must be available to the Team during the second segment to answer questions that the Team might have about the Improvement Backlog.
- It is up to the Team, acting solely on its own and without any direction from outside the Team, to figure out during the second segment how it will turn the selected Improvement Backlog into turning into an implemented and fully documented improvement. No one else is allowed to do anything but observe or answer questions seeking further information.
- The output of Phase 2 Planning is a list, called the Improvement Sprint Backlog, of tasks, task estimates, and assignments that will start the Team on the work of developing the improvements. The task list might not be complete, but it must be complete enough to reflect mutual commitment on the part of all Team members and to carry them through the first part of the Improvement Sprint, while the Team devises more tasks in the Improvement Sprint Backlog.

Process Improvement Sprint (2.5-3 Days)

1. Calculate Sprint Hours: 8 hours each per day
2. Sprint Start: MM/DD/YYYY
3. Sprint End: MM/DD/YYYY
4. Sprint Review: MM/DD/YYYY
5. Identify Backlog Item
6. Define Backlog Item Description
7. Determine Reward, Penalty, and Complexity
8. Create Sprint Tasks
9. Identify Point of Contact
10. Estimate Task in Minutes

7.04 Complete Improvement Sprint Tasks

Overview

During the Complete Improvement Sprint Tasks activity, Project Team Members complete the tasks they committed themselves to during planning. The Kaizen Facilitator is available to assist with any task. Improvement Sprints are iterative project cycles designed to implement an achievable improvement within two weeks. Project Sponsors and/or Process Owners can request as many Improvement Sprints as they feel necessary to achieve the desired results.

Objective

- Implement improvements
- Document results
- Learn and use other Lean tools

Estimated Time to Complete

120 to 240 Minutes per Improvement Sprint

Inputs (Resources required by the process)	Where/From
Improvement Sprint Backlog	7.03 Plan Improvement Backlog
Project Team Member(s)	Organization
Kaizen Facilitator	You
Failure Modes Effects Analysis	6.04 Perform FMEA
Current State Process Map	5.08 Define Sub-process Inputs and Outputs
Process Definition Document	5.08 Define Sub-process Inputs and Outputs
Lean Tools	Lean Body of Knowledge

Outputs (Deliverables from the process)	Possible Metrics
Implemented Improvements	Number of Improvements Implemented; Time to Implement
Reduced Process Risk	Primary Metrics Tracking
Updated Process Definition Document	Number of Updates to Process Definition Document
Updated Process Map	Number of Updates to Process Maps
Updated Failure Modes Effects Analysis	Changes in Risk to Input (RPN); Number of Changes to FMEA

Steps to Complete

1. Team Members complete identified tasks

2. Team Members tracks time spent of implementing improvements

3. Team Members update Kaizen Facilitator with issues

4. Kaizen Facilitator resolves issues

5. Kaizen Facilitator assists with the implementation of Lean Tools (e.g., 6S, Standardized Work, Kanban, etc.)

7.05 Review Improvement Sprint Results

Overview

During the Review Improvement Sprint Results activity the Kaizen Facilitator facilitates the review of implemented improvements. Project Team Members perform the formal presentation and review of implemented improvements to the Project Sponsor, Process Owner, and other stakeholders and interested parties. The Project Sponsor and/or Process Owner reviews the Project Team's results and compares the results to the done criteria for each improvement backlog item completed.

Objective

- Review improvement results
- Validate completion and done criteria
- Provide feedback and new opportunities

Estimated Time to Complete

60 Minutes

Inputs (Resources required by the process)	Where/From
Sprint Improvement Backlog	7.03 Plan Improvement Backlog
Kaizen Facilitator	You
Project Team Member(s)	Organization
Process Owner	Project Sponsor
Project Sponsor	Organization
Implemented Improvements	7.04 Complete Improvement Sprint Tasks
Reduced Process Risk	7.04 Complete Improvement Sprint Tasks
Updated Process Definition Document	7.04 Complete Improvement Sprint Tasks
Updated Process Map	7.04 Complete Improvement Sprint Tasks

Inputs (Resources required by the process)	Where/From
Updated Failure Modes Effects Analysis	7.04 Complete Improvement Sprint Tasks
Improvement Deliverable(s)	7.04 Complete Improvement Sprint Tasks

Outputs (Deliverables from the process)	Possible Metrics
Reviewed Improvements	Number of Improvements Implemented; Hours of Effort
Validated Improvement Deliverable(s)	Signed Off Deliverables; Updates to Improvement Backlog Items

Steps to Complete

1. Project Team Members review the Improvement Sprint Goals, Committed Improvement Sprint Backlog, and Completed Improvement Sprint Backlog

2. Project Team Members discuss what went well and what didn't go so well

3. Project Team Members review each improvement backlog item and present their improvement work to Project Sponsor and/or Process Owner

4. Process Owner or Project Sponsor updates Improvement Backlog based on feedback

5. Process Owner or Project Sponsor validates and recognizes improvements

7.06 Complete Improvement Sprint Retrospective

Overview

During the Complete Improvement Sprint Retrospective activity the Kaizen Facilitator facilitates a brief brainstorming session with Project Team Members to identify what went well during the improvement sprint, what didn't go so well, and what should be done different in future improvement sprints. Project Team Members also identify and document possible new opportunities for improvement backlog items.

Objective

- Improve communication between Project Team Members
- Sustain Kaizen activity
- Identify new improvement opportunities

Process Kaizen

Estimated Time to Complete

15 Minutes

Inputs (Resources required by the process)	Where/From
Improvement Sprint Backlog	7.04 Complete Improvement Sprint Tasks
Kaizen Facilitator	You
Project Team Member(s)	Organization
Reviewed Improvements	7.05 Review Improvement Sprint Results
Improvement Sprint Retrospective Template	Figure 7.06.01

Outputs (Deliverables from the process)	Possible Metrics
List of what went well	# of good items
List of what didn't go so well	# of bad items; # good items vs. bad items
List of possible new improvement backlog items	Improvement Backlog Item
Lists of what should be done differently during next improvement sprint	# Sprint Planning and Process Updates

Steps to Complete

1. Kaizen Facilitator kicks off meeting

2. Project Team Members discuss what went well during the improvement sprint

3. Project Team Members discuss what didn't go so well

4. Project Team Members discuss possible new improvement backlog items for future sprints

5. Project Team Members discuss what should be done differently during future improvement sprints

6. Kaizen Facilitator saves Improvement Sprint Retrospective Notes to a network Project Folder

Figure 7.06.01 Improvement Sprint Retrospective Template

Kaizen Event Improvement Sprint Retrospective Template	
What went well during the Kaizen Event or Kaizen activity?	
What didn't go so well during the Kaizen Event	

Kaizen Event Improvement Sprint Retrospective Template	
or Kaizen activity?	
What would you like to see done differently in future Kaizen Events or Kaizen activities?	

Appendix: Implementing Lean Improvements

Lean improvements focus on eliminating waste and streamlining the process to deliver more value to the end customer. As Lean Organizations progress, the Lean improvements build upon each other to transform the entire enterprise and all its processes. Lean improvements first focus on identifying and eliminating waste so that the process becomes more visible and defects can easily be identified. Quickly these Lean improvements lead specifying and focusing on value as well as focusing on the value stream and flow of activities and deliverables that are important to the customer.

Standard Work

What is Standard Work?

Standard Work is the foundation and framework for all future process improvements. All processes should be visual and easy to understand at a glance, by anybody in organization. By documenting the best, least waste, way to complete the current state process, organizations see improvements between 30-50%. By documenting standard work, you establish a baseline for continuous improvement as well as dramatically improve productivity and quality. Standard Work should be created by the people who are best at doing the work.

Why is Standard Work important?

- Helps establish a foundation of visual management and uncovers issues
- Prevents errors, defects and variation
- Improves team learning and communication
- Aligns workforce with clearly communicated organizational goals

Three Elements of Standard Work

Without Standard Work there can be no improvement. Standard Work helps form the foundation of continuous improvement. Without Standard Work abnormal events go undetected.

1. TAKT Time
   - Rate of customer consumption
   - Displayed in red on Standard Work Tools
2. Standard Work in Progress
   - The minimum work in progress needed to perform the operations and meet the production rate
3. Standard Work
   - Tasks and the sequence of those tasks

When should you use Standard Work?

- Standard Work sustains a consistent and reproducible method of delivering value
- Standard Work allows you understand the current state rather than having to constantly observe and verify it
- Establishes the important environment of coaching to standardized work

How to Complete Standard Work

If the Process needs to be defined:

1. Brainstorm high level process using Affinity Diagramming exercise and SIPOC
2. Define sub-process maps
3. Identify inputs and outputs for each activity box
4. Estimate how much time each activity should take and how much lag time is tolerable

If Process Maps have been completed:

1. Investigate each input and output and determine standards for each
   a. Validate all SOPs
   b. Validate Communication
   c. Validate Policies and Procedures
   d. Validate Tools/Systems Used
   e. Validate External Stakeholders
2. Provide links to each standard input and output on the Standard Work document
3. Create, Update, and Eliminate SOPs, Communication, Tools, etc. as necessary
4. Document the best possible steps to complete each activity (How we take each standard input documented and turn them into the standard outputs documented)
5. Provide a narrative description of the activity based on the steps to complete
6. Provide 2-3 bulleted objectives or goals for the activity (Why is this activity important? What are the key steps or take aways?)
7. Validate the Estimated time to complete

Process Kaizen

Example of Standard Work Combination Sheet

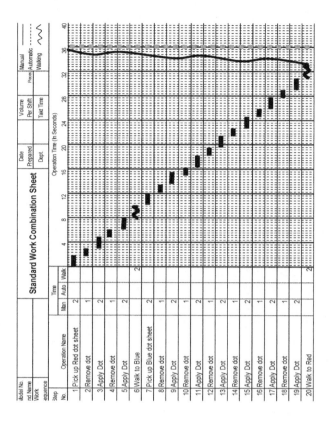

Steps to document Standard Work Layout

1. Document physical layout
2. Document operator work sequences
3. Document material flow
4. Establish Input Specifications and adherence to Standard Operations
5. Train operators in best, least waste, sequence of operations

Example of Standard Work Layout Sheet

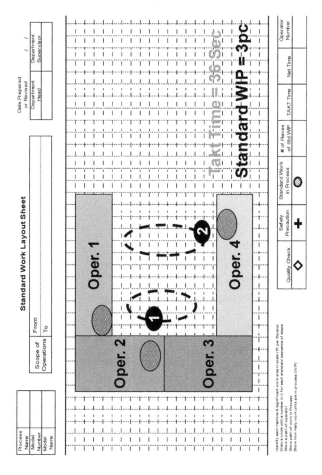

Training

What is Training?

During Kaizen Events, it is almost always found that lack of training and skills is a critical factor to overall process performance. Training is the foundation of Standard Work and continuous improvement.

Why is Training important?

- Develops skills and knowledge in setting standards
- Develops skills and knowledge in taking actions to improve standards
- Develops a sustainable mechanism for on boarding and inducting new workers
-

When should you use Training?

- When safety problems exist
- When there is a lack of qualifications in the workforce
- When methods of production are changing
- When rapid turnover exists
- When morale is low
- When you want to improve job methods
- When you want to plan and communicate production procedures to workers
- When you want to solve specific problems and promote Standard Work. By breaking down processes into defined activities with step to complete each activity, it is possible to clearly demonstrate the procedures to workers and observe worker attempts with effective coaching to get new workers up to speed quickly. This training should not be focused on your current workforce, but the long term development and training of your workforce as a whole – with a focus on new workers.

How to Complete Training

1. Develop Training to continuously reinforce documented Standard Work (Build modular training based on standard work components and from simple to complex tasks)
2. Show worker how to do the work component at full production speed to give a preliminary idea of how the job is done
3. Show the worker again, this time slowing down the demonstration to show each step. Explain critical points during this demonstration.
4. Demonstrate the work component again at full speed.
5. Facilitate a questions and answers session with the worker.
6. Observe worker completing the work component slowly.
7. Allow learner to repeat work component on his or her own while allowing questions via an Andon Cord process.
8. Develop visual mechanism to track training completed and training required
9. Document training completed and method of delivery
10. Track performance results for each work component and trained worker

Example of a Training Progress Board

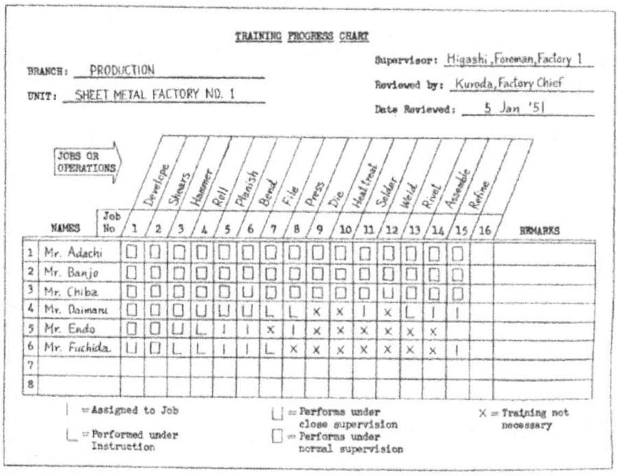

TRAINING PROGRESS CHART

BRANCH: PRODUCTION

UNIT: SHEET METAL FACTORY NO. 1

Supervisor: Higashi, Foreman, Factory 1

Reviewed by: Kuroda, Factory Chief

Date Reviewed: 5 Jan '51

JOBS OR OPERATIONS

	NAMES	Job No	1 Develope	2 Shears	3 Hammer	4 Roll	5 Planish	6 Bend	7 File	8 Press	9 Die	10 Heat treat	11 Solder	12 Weld	13 Rivet	14 Assemble	15 Refine	16	REMARKS
1	Mr. Adachi		□	□	□	□	□	□	□	□	□	□	□	□	□	□	□		
2	Mr. Banjo		□	□	□	□	□	□	□	□	□	□	□	□	□	□	□		
3	Mr. Chiba		□	□	□	□	□	⊔	□	□	□	□	□	⊔	□	□	□		
4	Mr. Daimaru		□	□	□	⊔	⊔	⊔	└	└	X	X	|	X	└	|	|		
5	Mr. Endo		□	□	⊔	└	|	|	X	|	X	X	X	X	X	X			
6	Mr. Fuchida		⊔	□	└	└	|	|	└	X	X	X	X	X	X	X	|		
7																			
8																			

| = Assigned to Job

└ = Performed under Instruction

⊔ = Performs under close supervision

□ = Performs under normal supervision

X = Training not necessary

Elimination of Wastes

What is Waste?

Waste is any activity that consumes resources and produces no added value to the product or service a customer receives. This is also known by the Japanese term "muda." Lean focuses on identifying and eliminating waste while focusing on the value being delivered to internal and external stakeholders.

Being able to distinguish between activities which add value and activities that do not is an important step of the improvement process. Kaizen teams should consistently ask "Is this something the customer would be willing to pay for?" And if the customer isn't aware of the activity, they most likely do not attribute value to the activity. Think of waste as adding cost without adding value.

Why is elimination of Waste important?

- Teaches workforce to identify and eliminate waste
- Teaches how to define and focus the value delivered to the customer
- Provides a uniform definition of value and waste
- Encourages stakeholders to walk and improve processes
- Things going through processes are usually 99% idle.

When should you eliminate Waste?

- To recognize wasted activities and motions in processes
- To reduce waiting periods
- To streamline process steps
- To improve customer service, responsiveness and operational flexibility
- To improve workforce satisfaction

How to measure waste

- **Inventory** – All physical goods on hand that are to be consumed or transformed into a product. Inventory includes raw materials, all work in process (WIP) and goods used in manufacturing, and finished goods.
- **Inventory Turn** – Annual cost of goods sold divided by average inventory in dollars.
- **Cycle Time** – The amount of human time needed to accomplish the standard work sequence for one product or service
- **Productivity** – Total labor hours to produce one unit
- **Space** – The area utilized to produce a standard product or service.
- **Setup Time** – The time required for a specific machine, resources, work center, or line to convert from the last good piece of a lot A to the first good piece of lot B
- **Lead Time** – The total time from internal/external customer order to delivery of the desired product or service
- **People Travel** - The distance in feet that a person travels to perform a certain task or series of tasks. This includes the retrieval of tools, materials and supplies.

- **Product Travel** – The distance in feet that a product travels through the manufacturing process
- **Rework** – Number of defective parts corrected.
- **Crew Size** – The number of employees support the processing sequence.

How to document waste

1. Document each unique process step
2. Categorize the process type (e.g., handling, inspection, transportation, etc.)
3. Document process step times
4. Document comments

How to eliminate waste

1. Identify Non Value Added Activities from Process Maps and Waste Maps
2. Identify lengthy (over 1 minute) Process Lag Times from Process Maps

Example of Waste Map

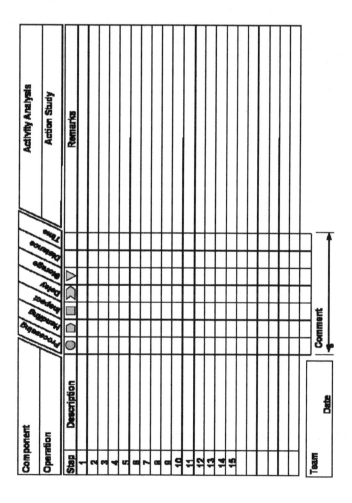

6S Housekeeping and Organization

What is 6S?

6S (AKA 5S and 5S+1) is a process for creating and maintaining and organized, clean, safe and high performance workplace. 6S is at the foundation of the Lean and Kaizen methodologies and is critical to workplace organization and housekeeping.

Poor workplace conditions lead to waste such as extra motions to avoid obstacles, extra time spent searching for things, and delays and rework due to defects, machine failures, or accidents.

6S helps teams standardize a simple process to improve the workplace, improve communication, and enable a safer and more effective operation.

Why is 6S important?

- Lean Organizations develop beginning with 6S
- Workers need understand their role and how they contribute to the organization
- 6S is critical to future Lean improvement efforts
- Reduces wasted time, materials and costs
- Simplifies the work environment

When should you do 6S?

- Space is crowded with parts and tools
- Equipment is dirty and the workplace unorganized
- Too many "things" packed into storage spaces
- Work areas used as storage spaces instead of work spaces
- Information is posted and available, yet nobody knows what is going on
- Accidents are just waiting to happen
- Administrative work areas are unorganized or cluttered

How to Complete 6S

1. Determine what the definition of necessary is
2. Establish who decides what to keep and what to get rid of
3. Determine if there is anything off limits
4. Determine what should happen to the items that are removed (Holding Area)
5. Prepare boxes and storage areas
6. Sort and Inventory everything in the target area
7. Separate and red tag the items that are unnecessary or in the wrong location
8. Keep only what is necessary and remove everything else from the work area
9. Create and use a common storage area for items that are not used daily
10. Determine the outcome of unnecessary items
11. Determine how often the Sort activity should be done

12. Select problems or problem areas to improve
13. Move items to where they belong
14. Make it obvious where things belong
    Ask 4 questions:

    I. What is this?
    II. Should I keep, store, or discard it?
    III. If I need it, how many should I keep?
    IV. If I need it, how often do I use it?
15. Determine cleaning targets and assignments
16. Determine cleaning methods
17. Perform initial cleaning and inspection
    Ask 5 questions

    I. Is this a dangerous situation?
    II. Are there equipment, materials, or environmental hazards in the area?
    III. Is anyone in my area doing anything that could be dangerous or is not consistent with safety practices?
    IV. Is everyone in my areas wearing the required personal protective equipment?
    V. What am I going to do about it if I answered YES to any of the above 4 questions?
18. Document standards for Sort, Straighten and Shine activities
19. Integrate standard activities into daily work
20. Assign accountability to each team member, team lead, and manager
21. Establish checklists and schedules for each activity
22. Provide pictures of the ideal state
23. Use pictures of your results
24. Schedule 6S Audits for the year
25. Establish 6S problem solving procedures for day-to-day work
26. Cleary define times during the day for 6S activities
27. Schedule next 6S event for work area for continuous improvement
28. Pursue perfection of 6S awareness within work area

Setup Reduction/Elimination

What is Setup Time?

Setup Time is the time from a last finished part of a run within a process until the first part of the next run made at a normal rate.

What is Setup Reduction/Elimination?

Setup reduction is a team based improvement activity that provides a systematic approach in order to significantly reduce setup and changeover times. Setup reduction is designed to maximize the amount of time a give process or machine is up and running while minimizing the time it take to change from one process to another. Setup reduction focuses on understanding current state setup and changeover times, identifying and classifying the tasks and times within the process, and moving as many tasks as possible to before or after the actual change over.

Why is Setup Reduction important?

- Reduces overtime
- Increases equipment utilization and effectiveness
- Increases process capability and capacity
- Reduces batch sizes
- Dramatically shortens lead time

What are the key steps to Setup Reduction/Elimination?

1. Implement 6S prior to starting Setup Reduction
2. Document/verity current state process with categorized tasks and times
3. Separate internal and external process tasks and activities
4. Define and separate the work to be performed while the machine is stopped from the work that can be done while the machine is in production.
   a. Reduce internal setup by doing more work externally (preparation of dies, transfer of parts, etc.)
   b. Reduce the remaining internal setup by eliminating adjustments, standardizing changing parts, etc.
   c. Reduce the total time of both internal and external work.
5. Standardize all setup operations

How to streamline internal and external activities

1. Establish parallel operations for internal and external tasks and times
2. Eliminate adjustment requirements of equipment and establish fool proofed orientation
3. Minimize clamping and securing points in favor of one turn attachment
4. Standardize functional tool dimensions and reduce or eliminate tool adjustment

Process Kaizen

5. Minimize standardized securing and guarding
6. Reduce tool, equipment and material transportation using point of use material/tool storage and adjustable conveyors and trolleys
7. Standardize equipment, tools, and workplace organization with visual controls

Example Setup Data Collection Sheet

SETUP DATA SHEETS	DATE			
	SHIFT			
Process	NAME			
TASK	START TIME	END TIME	DURATION	COMMENTS

Continuous Setup Reduction Cycle

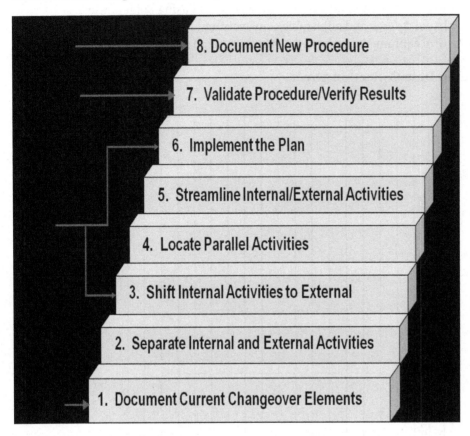

What is Total Productive Maintenance?

Total Productive Maintenance (AKA TPM) is a continuous improvement program for operation and maintenance of equipment through small, targeted, group and individual activities. The vision of TPM is "we maintain machines ourselves."

TPM involves maintenance teams, the operators, and management to make it easy, with visual instructions, to reduce waste and improve overall equipment effectiveness. TPM provides a baseline to measure the overall health of equipment and to identify critical inputs that are influencing process performance.

What types of equipment require Total Productive Maintenance?

- Computers
- Scanners
- Copiers, Printers, Fax Machine
- Most Machines
- Pretty much any equipment used in the process

Why is Total Productive Maintenance important?

- Resolves the operational conflict of "I operate it, you fix it!"
- Eliminates breakdowns and defects causes by machines and equipment
- Chronic equipment breakdown and failure is a critical factor to waste and process instability
- Provides extended times between breakdowns and failures and faster times to repair
- Makes equipment always available for operation
- Keeps things clean and safe

When should you do Total Productive Maintenance?

- When parts consistently experience wear and tear
- When parts deform due to deflection and distortion
- When dirt and dust accumulate
- When lubrication and other chemicals are used
- When air, electrical, or water intake or discharge rates change
- When damage occurs
- When filters, belts, hoses and other recurring maintenance is not regularly completed
- When workers don't have enough time to correct problems and improve reliability
- When equipment experiences long downtimes as a result of sudden break down
- When lengthy setup times create downtime
- When uneven work flow or short stoppages are being causes by defective product
- When equipment is running slower that it was designed
- When there is a contestant stopping and starting of equipment

Process Kaizen

How to complete Total Productive Maintenance

1. Start with 6S Event to assist in identification of necessary and unnecessary items
2. Identify all equipment used in the production process
3. Establish Spare Parts Management Plan
4. Establish Emergency Breakdown Response Plan
5. Identify all recurring and special maintenance
6. Establish necessary tools and equipment to perform identified maintenance
7. Schedule recurring and special maintenance and plan procurement and delivery of necessary equipment and materials
8. Develop new equipment maintenance specifications for each identified
9. Establish a mechanism or audit plan for monitoring machine conditions
10. Document Preventative Maintenance Plan
    a. Daily Operator Maintenance
    b. Cleaning
    c. Checking
    d. Lubricating
    e. Tightenting
11. Establish Corrective Maintenance and Troubleshooting actions
12. Establish minimum and maximum breakdown maintenance downtimes
13. Establish operator logs for operator maintenance
14. When equipment fails, leverage the Failure Modes Effect Analysis exercise to determine failure modes, root causes, and corrective actions.
15. Establish Operator Performed Maintenance checklist
16. Conduct Operator Maintenance skills training
17. Track training and results

Visual Controls & Kanban

What are Visual Controls and Kanban?

Visual controls allow anybody on the production floor (even visitors) to understand the current goals and conditions of all processes. Visual controls communicate important information, in the form of standards, goals and current performance.

Kanban is a Japanese term meaning "signal" or "visual record" and is used within the Just in Time system to signal a cycle of replenishment for production and materials. Kanban helps maintain an orderly and efficient material flow throughout the process.

Why are Visual Controls and Kanban important?

- Reduces raw material inventory
- Reduces finished goods inventory
- Supports a stable workforce
- Improves quality
- Increases production flexibility and communication
- Improves responsiveness

When should you do Visual Controls and Kanban?

- To identify abnormal conditions immediately
- To display standardized methods
- To communicate performance meastures and corrective actions
- To communicate and compare TAKT Time to Cycle time
- To display standard work sequences

The five forms of Visual Control

1. Visual Standardized Work Methods
    a. Standard Work Combination Sheet
    b. Standard Work Layout
    c. Safety Rules
    d. Part/Process Tolerances
    e. Set-up Parameters
    f. Operation Instructions
    g. Part/Component Quality Standard Board
    h. Packaging/Product Display Instructions
2. Visual Production/Process Control
    a. Goals must be realistic and attainable
    b. Use Takt time and cycle time
    c. Team should enter their own data
    d. Precisely defined quotas
    e. Standardized color system

         f. Identify exceptions to plan
         g. Delays
         h. Material shortages
         i. Equipment availability
         j. Manpower shortages
   3. Visual Quality Control
         a. Objective evaluation of performance (scrap, rework, DPMO, etc. in <u>real</u> time)
         b. Statistical Process Control
         c. Visual Signals (Andons)
         d. Pass/Fail templates or gauges
         e. Problem recording and resolution system
         f. Display of defects
         g. Detection is good
   4. Visual Process Indicators
         a. What's the score?
         b. Each inning
         c. Each out or run
         d. Real time indicators
         e. Leading vs. Trailing
         f. Objective measures
         g. Scrap
         h. Rework
         i. Delivery
         j. Productivity
         k. Preventative Maintenance (PM
   5. Visual 6S
         a. Housekeeping audits
         b. Self-maintained
         c. Colors/shapes/pictures
         d. "Hospital" standard

How to Complete Visual Controls

1. Identify a target area using 6S audit results and any current state process maps
2. Decide on specific visual strategies to use for improvement
3. Develop and apply visual controls
      a. Mark symbolic boundaries with lines
      b. Show where items belong
      c. Show which directions to walk and where people should and should not stand
4. Establish a mechanism and process for updating visual controls
5. Engage and train workers

Tradition Kanban Solutions

1. Production (AKA "Make") Kanbans
2. Withdrawal (AKA "Take") Kanbans
3. Inventory Control Kanbans (e.g., two bin inventory and waterspiders)
4. Broadcast Kanban (electronic signal or sound at start of production)

How to Complete Kanban

1. Start with end of downstream processes to allow for necessary parts and products to be withdrawn in the necessary quantities at the correct point in time
2. Follow the process upstream and have each step produce the necessary quantities for downstream steps
3. Establish Kanban visual controls between each to prevent unnecessary transportation and overproduction
4. For each movement of parts of product, setup Kanban visual controls to be part of that movement
5. Establish a visual mechanism to reject and correct defective parts or products prior to them being moved to the next step in the process
6. Fine-tune and minimize the number of Kanbans necessary for the process, while continuing to reduce cycle time and inventory.

TAKT Time

What is TAKT Time?

TAKT time is used to set the production rate within the organization to the rate at which the customer demands the product or service. The bottom line is that the customer determine TAKT time by the demand placed on your product or service. Understand that demand timing at a day to day basis allows organizations increase productivity by aligning operator cycle times to customer TAKT times, while dramatically reducing inventory and lead time. Without this pace setting concept, processes will typically create more than is needed, before it's needed, of stuff that is not needed.

Why is TAKT Time important?

- Better work balance
- Constant flow
- Have control to make what we need
- Provides a method to keep score
- Can change quickly to meet the customers' demands
- Visual WIP control

When should you use TAKT Time?

- To develop a rate of production equal to customer demand
- To develop a detailed view of how things are going, minute by minute
- To quickly determine the minimum number of resources to get a job done
- To compare what should happen to what is really happening
- To have clear visibility at all level of the organization into cycle times

How to implement TAKT Time

1. Determine the time period to be used for TAKT calculation (e.g., shift, day, week – no less than one minute)
2. Determine how often you will need to recalculate TAKT time
3. Determine available production time per time period
4. Determine the total production requirements per time period
5. Observe the cycle time for all process tasks and activities, break each into the lowest repeatable element
6. Record the time it takes to perform each work element
7. Build percent loading chart to compare operator cycle time to TAKT time
8. Balance each operators work load to match established TAKT time (swapping tasks and cross training when appropriate)
9. Determine the Standard Work in Progress for process by specifying the minimum amount of material that must be in process to allow for proper flow of operation to TAKT time (Cycle Time / TAKT time)

Process Kaizen

Example of TAKT Time Calculation Worksheet

Takt Time = Net Operating Time Available / Customer Demand

Net Operating Time available:

_____ # hours/time period

_____ minutes/time period (# hours/time period) X 60 minutes/hour

_____ breaks (minutes)

_____ clean up time (minutes)

_____ set up time (minutes)

total = _____ available production minutes X 60 = _____ Available Production Seconds

Customer Demand:

_____ Customer Requirement (pallets)

Takt Time = Available Production Seconds / Customer Requirements

Takt Time = _____ seconds/pallet

Example of a Time Observation Form

[Time Observation Form: a blank grid with columns labeled 1–10 for Points Observed, rows for Item No., Component Task, Component Task Time, and Time for 1 Cycle. Header fields include Process for Observation, Date & Time, Observer, Team, and Analysis #.]

Steps to Complete a Time Observation Form

1. Identify work elements to be observed and timed
2. Document steps each operator completes to finish one cycle of work
3. Determine observations points for steps to observe and measure
4. Time each element in seconds (with a minimum of ten measured observations)
5. Ask operator to perform an additional ten operations
6. Calculate average cycle times – process times and lag times
7. Identify best repeatable cycle times for each operation
8. Establish benchmark for operation cycle times
9. Communicate visual standard work tied to cycle times and train operators in best practices

Continuous Flow

What is Continuous Flow?

Continuous Flow is a transactional environment that eliminates all starts and stops in the process, in favor of a continuous flow of activities and deliverables based on customer TAKT time. In this model, all Non-value added activities have been eliminated and once information or a product has started its process route, it completes in one single flow. This is traditionally accomplished using the Lean improvements discussed above – especially well defined processes and standard work and visual controls to display the health of the process.

Why is Continuous Flow important?

- Dramatically improves quality because work is passed directly to the next process with no defects
- Eliminates Non-value added activities and common forms of waste
- Root causes can be immediately identified and solved in real time
- Increases the morale of workforce by making value of work more visible
- Dramatically reduces cycle time and lead time while improving process flexibility
- Eliminate Work in Process (WIP)

When should you use Continuous Flow?

- To develop a system intolerant of production abnormalities
- Simplifies the workplace and reduces documentation and processing steps
- To Reduce lead time and operational flexibility
- To improve the layout of work areas
- To eliminate excess inventory and other wasste

The Seven Flows of Production

1. People
2. Parts/Product
3. Equipment/Tools
4. Information
5. Material
6. Time
7. New Ideas

How to Complete Continuous Flow

1. Production in Specialized Departments
2. Production in Product Cell
3. Production with One-Piece Flow
4. Production in Product Cell with One-Piece Flow and Separation of Man/Machine

Just in Time

What is Just in Time?

Principles of Just in Time systems and processes first focus on the pace of TAKT time, then on creating a flow of processes to deliver on that TAKT time, and finally by incorporating a streamlined pull system. Since variation is not tolerated within Just in Time systems, it is imperative to have all material management, supplier management, production and design, processes standardized prior to pursuing Just in Time improvements.

Just in Time is a project and inventory control technique to produce just what is needed, when it is needed in the amount it is needed.

Three Key Elements to Just in Time

1. Flow (continuous)
Flow of products in level manner through the production operations. Ideally one-piece flow at and between processes. Intent of continuous flow production is to increase the velocity of products (reduced cycle time), and make the production cycle reliable and predictable.

2. Pull
A customer-driven system that produces and moves products or services only when the customer needs them.

3. TAKT Time
The daily "heartbeat" of production. The amount of time allowed to produce one unit of product, based on the customer rate of demand and the available work time per day.

Why is Just in Time important?

- Identifies production abnormalities for continuous improvement
- Improves operational flexibility, communication and delivery time
- Dramatically reduces inventory by 50-90%
- Supports the focus on cost out, quality in.

The Critical Inputs of Just in Time

- Material Management
- Total Productive Maintenance
- Facility Layout
- Pull Process
- Quick Process Changeover
- Management leadership
- Management – Labor cooperation
- Multi–functional/multi – skilled employees
- Focus on flow of production/process

- Quality at the source
- Visual Controls

When should you use Just in Time?

- To create an environment for Standard Operations
- To allow for multi – process – handling workers
- To make material management more visual
- To create capacity and the opportunity to redeploy workers for business growth

How to Complete Just in Time

1. Define TAKT Time
2. Create flow, line of sight, balanced work, visual controls
3. Create streamlined layout based on flow
4. Document standard work for pull discipline based on TAKT Time
5. Establish and communicate a predictable flow, WIP, and lead time

Tracking and Reporting Progress and Performance Improvement

After improvements have been implemented, it is important to communicate those improvements. It's also vital to immediately start tracking the identified critical input and output metrics.

Control Plans allow project sponsors and stakeholders to quickly understand the current state of the process, improvements implemented, team participation, and a recording of period performance, to which project sponsors and stakeholders ultimately react.

To successfully "close out" a Kaizen Event, the Kaizen Event facilitator should formally meet with the project sponsor and stakeholders to build consensus around the Control Plan, including an in depth review of the improvements, agreement on the established controls for inputs and outputs, audit schedules are reviewed, and training is discussed.

What is a Control Plan?

Control Plans are documents that provide a point of reference to the critical inputs and outputs of the process and maintain operational details for how to react when output characteristics are not meeting expectations in terms of time, cost, or quality.

Control Plans build operational discipline and standardization around preventative maintenance, output reaction plans, training plans, control documentation, audits and checklists, change and version control, and control charts used track the progress of performance.

What are the common components of a Control Plan?

1. Control Charts
2. Long term Measurement System Analysis
3. Reaction Plan
4. Visual Standardized Work w/ SOPs
5. Change and Revision Control
6. Process Maps
7. Failure Modes Effects Analysis
8. Checklists and Audits
9. Preventative Maintenance
10. Long term Training Plan

Why use Control Plans?

- Empower lower ownership and control of processes
- Makes processes more visible with timely information
- Makes is clear what do to when a process is out of tolerance
- Provides Standard Work for process owners and stakeholders
- Establishes frequent measurement of process performance

- Tells process owners what inputs need to be controlled at to what level

How to complete a Control Plan

1. Identify the Process Area to be controlled
2. Provide a direct link to Kaizen Event deliverables (e.g., process maps, C&E, FMEA)
3. List each critical factor from the FMEA and identify the process steps in which the input occurs
4. Identify each key input and each key output
5. Document assessment criteria and any identified upper or lower specification limits
6. Document the steps to measure the input or output – Including:
    a. Sample Size
    b. Frequency of Measure
    c. Who Measures
    d. Where Measurements are recorded
    e. Corrective actions when out of tolerance
    f. Reference to SOP
7. Establish a formal revision control mechanism that prohibits changing control plan and identifies who can improve the process
8. Establish audits based on data collection frequency requirements
9. Establish training plan to appropriately train all future workers and managers in the process
    a. Operations steps
    b. Policies
    c. Training Tracker
    d. Onboarding
    e. Continuous Improvement

Example of a Control Plan

Sub Process	Sub Process Step	CTQ		Specification Characteristic	Specification/ Requirement		Measurement Method	Sample Size	Frequency	Who Measures	Where Recorded	Decision Rule/ Corrective Action	SOP Reference
		KPOV	KPIV		USL	LSL							

Control Plan header fields: Process Name, Customer (Int/Ext), Location, Area, Prepared by, Approved by, Approved by, Approved by, Page __ of __, Document No, Revision Date, Supercedes.

What is a Kaizen Event Summary Presentation?

Project tracking plays an important role in the success of Kaizen Events. A Kaizen Event Summary Presentation is designed to communicate the project description, the critical factors identified, the improvements implemented at the ongoing performance results based on implemented improvements.

The Kaizen Event Summary Presentation also provides clear documentation on the completion of each Kaizen Event deliverable and the tools used to identify improvements and deliver results.

Kaizen Event Summary Presentations should be reviewed with process owners and stakeholders and updated by process owners.

Why are Kaizen Event Summary Presentations important?

- Communicates to process owners which inputs need to be controlled
- Describes what the output metrics should be if the inputs are controlled
- Describes specific actions taken and improvement implemented during the Kaizen Event
- Tracks the progress of performance after improvement has been implemented

When should a Kaizen Event Summary Presentation be completed?

- To communicate the improvements implemented during the Kaizen Event
- To communicate what is left to be done
- To communicate roles and responsibility changes within the process
- To Communicate the progress of performance
- To generate team buy-in and process handoff to stakeholders

How to Develop a Kaizen Event Summary Presentation

1. Document key project descriptors
   a. Location
   b. Project Name
   c. Kaizen Facilitator
   d. Project Sponsor
   e. Project Team
   f. Completion Date
2. Describe the top 5-7 critical inputs identified and how each was failing with root causes
3. Describe the top 5-7 implemented improvements
4. Document the targeted improvement goal
5. Track the periodic (daily, weekly, monthly) progress of the primary metric
6. Provide Appendix of links to each Kaizen Event deliverable
   a. Charter
   b. SIPOC
   c. Process Maps
   d. Process Definition Document
   e. Cause and Effect Analysis
   f. Failure Modes Effects Analysis
   g. Improvement Backlog
   h. Improvements Folder
   i. Kaizen Event Summary Presentation

Example of a Kaizen Event Summary

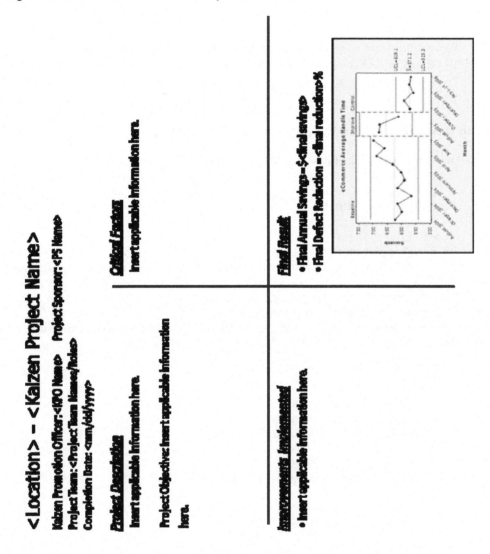

Glossary of Terms

A

Alignment: Actions to ensure that a process or activity supports the organization's strategy, goals and objectives.

Audit: The on-site verification activity, such as inspection or examination, of a process or quality system, to ensure compliance to requirements. An audit can apply to an entire organization or might be specific to a function, process or production step.

Affinity Diagramming: A business tool used to organize ideas and data. The tool is commonly used to generate a large number of ideas stemming from brainstorming to be sorted into groups for review and analysis.

Andon Cord: Any visual and/or auditory signal that allows anyone in a work area to understand, at a glance, the current status of the process within the work area. Andon Cords are primarily used to signal that a defect has been identified in the process or that a stakeholder within the process needs help. We bring attention to quality or process issues as they occur through the use of Andon Cords.

B

Balanced scorecard: A management system that provides feedback on both internal business processes and external outcomes to continuously improve strategic performance and results.

Balancing the line (AKA, Production Balancing or Smoothing): The process of evenly distributing both the quantity and variety of work across available work time, avoiding overburden and underuse of resources. This eliminates bottlenecks and downtime, which translates into shorter flow time.

Baseline Measurement: The beginning point, based on an evaluation of output over a period of time, used to determine the process parameters prior to any improvement effort; the basis against which change is measured.

Batch and queue: Producing more than one piece and then moving the pieces to the next operation before they are needed.

Benchmarking: A technique in which a company measures its performance against that of best in class organizations or groups, determines how those organizations or groups achieved their performance levels and uses the information to improve its own performance. Subjects that can be benchmarked include strategies, operations and processes.

Benefit-cost analysis: An examination of the relationship between the monetary cost of implementing an improvement and the monetary value of the benefits achieved by the improvement, both within the same time period.

Best practice: A superior method or innovative practice that contributes to the improved performance of an organization, usually recognized as best by other peer organizations.

Breakthrough improvement: A dynamic, decisive movement to a new, higher level of performance.

C

Capability: The total range of inherent variation in a stable process determined by using data from control charts.

Cause and Effect Analysis: An analysis tool that finds the few critical inputs that have the largest impacts on process outputs.

Champion: A business leader or senior manager who ensures resources are available for training and projects, and who is involved in periodic project reviews; also an executive who supports and addresses Lean and Kaizen organizational issues.

Change agent: An individual from within or outside an organization who facilitates change in the organization; might be the initiator of the change effort, but not necessarily.

Changeover: The process for converting a line or machine from running one product to another. The terms setup and changeover are sometimes used interchangeably, however this usage is incorrect. Setup is only one component of changeover.

Continuous improvement (CI): Sometimes called continual improvement. The ongoing improvement of products, services or processes through incremental and breakthrough improvements.

Control Chart: Time ordered data that is evaluated for runs, trends, and patterns that are unlikely to have come from the baseline process, identifying unexpected variation and expected variation using mean, standard deviation, upper specification limits, and lower specification limits.

Cost of poor quality (COPQ): The costs associated with providing poor quality products or services. There are four categories: internal failure costs (costs associated with defects found before the customer receives the product or service), external failure costs (costs associated with defects found after the customer receives the product or service), appraisal costs (costs incurred to determine the degree of conformance to quality requirements) and prevention costs (costs incurred to keep failure and appraisal costs to a minimum).

Counter Metric: Counter metrics are secondary metrics used in process improvement projects to ensure that particular areas of the process are not negatively impacted by Kaizen Event improvements.

Critical to Satisfaction Measures: Also commonly referred to as CT Flowdown

Cross functional: A term used to describe a process or an activity that crosses the boundary between functions. A cross functional team consists of individuals from more than one organizational unit or function.

CT Flowdown: See "Critical to Satisfaction Measures"

Customer: Any internal or external process stakeholder who receives an output of the process.

Customer relationship management (CRM): A strategy for learning more about customers' needs and behaviors to develop stronger relationships with them. It brings together information about customers, sales, marketing effectiveness, responsiveness and market trends. It helps businesses use technology and human resources to gain insight into the behavior of customers and the value of those customers.

Customer satisfaction: The result of delivering a product or service that meets customer requirements.

Cycle: A sequence of operations repeated regularly.

Cycle time: The time required to complete one cycle of an operation. If cycle time for every operation in a complete process can be reduced to equal takt time, products can be made in single-piece flow. Also see "takt time."

D

Daily Kaizen: A standard method of managing and improving the value stream that empowers associates to focus on continuous improvement in their everyday work. Daily Kaizen uses simple yet robust lean management systems and a pragmatic comparison of the current state with the envisioned ideal state and enables workers to identify and fix problems.

Data: A set of collected facts. There are two basic kinds of numerical data: measured or variable data, such as "16 ounces," "4 miles" and "0.75 inches;" and counted or attribute data, such as "162 defects."

Data Collection Plan: A plan that identifies what to measure, the type of measure, the type of data, the operational definition of the data, a general plan for extracting, sampling and analyzing the data.

Defect: A product's or service's nonfulfillment of an intended requirement or reasonable expectation for use, including safety considerations. There are four classes of defects: class 1, very serious, leads directly to severe injury or catastrophic economic loss; class 2, serious, leads directly to significant injury or significant economic loss; class 3, major, is related to major problems with respect to intended normal or reasonably foreseeable use; and class 4, minor, is related to minor problems with respect to intended normal or reasonably foreseeable use. Also see "blemish," "imperfection" and "nonconformity."

Defective: A defective unit; a unit of product that contains one or more defects with respect to the quality characteristic(s) under consideration.

Delighter: A feature of a product or service that a customer does not expect to receive but that gives pleasure to the customer when received. Also called an "exciter."

Deming cycle: Another term for the plan-do-study-act cycle. Walter Shewhart created it (calling it the plan-do-check-act cycle), but W. Edwards Deming popularized it, calling it plan-do-study-act. Also see "plan-do-check-act cycle.

Dependability: The degree to which a product is operable and capable of performing its required function at any randomly chosen time during its specified operating time, provided that the product is available at the start of that period. (Nonoperation related influences are not included.) Dependability can be expressed by the ratio: time available divided by (time available + time required).

Design on Experiment: A planned set of tests of the outputs with one or more inputs, each at two or more settings to determine if any factor or combination of factors affect the variation on the output, affect both the average and the variation of the output, or have not effect on the output.

Discrete Data: Information that is traditionally counted in whole numbers is known as "discrete data." Examples of discrete data include count, true or false, yes or no, and most other

DMADV: A data driven quality strategy for designing products and processes, it is an integral part of a Six Sigma quality initiative. It consists of five interconnected phases: define, measure, analyze, design and verify.

DMAIC: A data driven quality strategy for improving processes and an integral part of a Six Sigma quality initiative. DMAIC is an acronym for define, measure, analyze, improve and control.

DPMO: Defect per million opportunities for error. A defect is considered as a nonconformance of a quality characteristic.

E

Effect: The result of an action being taken; the expected or predicted impact when an action is to be taken or is proposed.

Efficiency: The ratio of the output to the total input in a process.

Efficient: A term describing a process that operates effectively while consuming minimal resources (such as labor and time).

Eight wastes: Taiichi Ohno originally enumerated seven wastes (muda) and later added underutilized people as the eighth waste commonly found in physical production. The eight are: 1. overproduction ahead of demand; 2. waiting for the next process, worker, material or equipment; 3. unnecessary transport of materials (for example, between functional areas of facilities, or to or from a stockroom or warehouse); 4. over-processing of parts due to poor tool and product design; 5. inventories more than the absolute minimum; 6. unnecessary movement by employees during the course of their work (such as to look for parts, tools, prints or help); 7. production of defective parts; 8. under-utilization of employees' brainpower, skills, experience and talents.

Eighty-twenty (80-20): A term referring to the Pareto principle, which was first defined by J. M. Juran in 1950. The principle suggests most effects come from relatively few causes; that is, 80% of the effects come from 20% of the possible causes. Also see "Pareto chart."

Empowerment: A condition in which employees have the authority to make decisions and take action in their work areas without prior approval. For example, an operator can stop a production process if he or she detects a problem, or a customer service representative can send out a replacement product if a customer calls with a problem.

Error Proofing (See Mistake Proofing): Use of production or design features to prevent the manufacture or passing downstream a nonconforming product; also known as "error proofing."

External customer: A person or organization that receives a product, service or information but is not part of the organization supplying it. Also see "internal customer."

F

Facilitator: A specifically trained person who functions as a teacher, coach and moderator for a group, team or organization.

Failure: The inability of an item, product or service to perform required functions on demand due to one or more defects.

Failure Modes Effects Analysis: A systematized group of activities to recognize and evaluate the potential failure of a product or process and its effects, identify actions that could eliminate or reduce the occurrence of the potential failure and document the process.

Five S's (AKA 5S or 6S): Five Japanese terms beginning with "s" used to create a workplace suited for visual control and lean production. Seiri means to separate needed tools, parts and instructions from unneeded materials and to remove the unneeded ones. Seiton means to neatly arrange and identify parts and tools for ease of use. Seiso means to conduct a cleanup campaign. Seiketsu means to conduct seiri, seiton and seiso daily to maintain a workplace in perfect condition. Shitsuke means to form the habit of always following the first four S's.

Five whys: A technique for discovering the root causes of a problem and showing the relationship of causes by repeatedly asking the question, "Why?"

Flowchart: A graphical representation of the steps in a process. Flowcharts are drawn to better understand processes. One of the "seven tools of quality" (see listing).

14 Points: W. Edwards Deming's 14 management practices to help companies increase their quality and productivity: 1. create constancy of purpose for improving products and services; 2. adopt the new philosophy; 3. cease dependence on inspection to achieve quality; 4. end the practice of awarding business on price alone; instead, minimize total cost by working with a single supplier; 5. improve constantly and forever every process for planning, production and service; 6. institute training on the job; 7. adopt and institute leadership; 8. drive out fear; 9. break down barriers between staff areas; 10. eliminate slogans, exhortations and targets for the workforce; 11. eliminate numerical quotas for the workforce and numerical goals for management; 12. remove barriers that rob people of pride of workmanship, and eliminate the annual rating or merit system; 13. institute a rigorous program of education and self-improvement for everyone; 14. put everybody in the company to work to accomplish the transformation. Frequency distribution (statistical): A table that graphically presents a large volume of data so the central tendency (such as the average or mean) and distribution are clearly displayed.

G

Gap analysis: The comparison of a current condition to the desired state.

Goal: A broad statement describing a desired future condition or achievement without being specific about how much and when.

Green Belt (GB): An employee who has been trained in the Lean Six Sigma improvement method and will lead a process improvement or quality improvement team as part of his or her full-time job.

Groupthink: A situation in which critical information is withheld from the team because individual members censor or restrain themselves, either because they believe their concerns are not worth discussing or because they are afraid of confrontation.

H

Hawthorne effect: The concept that every change results (initially, at least) in increased productivity.

Histogram: A graphical representation showing a visual impression of the distribution of data. It is an estimate of the probability distribution of a continuous variable.

House of quality: A product planning matrix, somewhat resembling a house, which is developed during quality function deployment and shows the relationship of customer requirements to the means of achieving these requirements.

Hypothesis Testing: A procedure for testing a claim about a population parameter using samples of data to confidently answer practical questions about the population of data.

I

Idea Board: The Daily Kaizen Idea Board is designed for employees to easily provide ideas that help make the process more effective and efficient and everyone's lives easier.

Improvement: The positive effect of a process change effort.

In-control process: A process in which the statistical measure being evaluated is in a state of statistical control; in other words, the variations among the observed sampling results can be attributed to a constant system of chance causes. Also see "out-of-control process."

Incremental improvement: Improvement implemented on a continual basis.

Indicators: Established measures to determine how well an organization is meeting its customers' needs and other operational and financial performance expectations.

Inputs: The products, services and material obtained from suppliers to produce the outputs delivered to customers.

Inspection: Measuring, examining, testing and gauging one or more characteristics of a product or service and comparing the results with specified requirements to determine whether conformity is achieved for each characteristic.

Intermediate customers: Organizations or individuals who operate as distributors, brokers or dealers between the supplier and the consumer or end user.

Internal customer: The recipient (person or department) within an organization of another person's or department's output (product, service or information).

Inventory: In lean, the money invested to purchase things an organization intends to sell.

J

Just in Case Mentality: A fear based mentality that establishes backup plan and alternatives rather than planning against assumptions, risks, and obstacles.

Just-in-time (JIT) manufacturing: An optimal material requirement planning system for a manufacturing process in which there is little or no manufacturing material inventory on hand at the manufacturing site and little or no incoming inspection.

Just-in-time (JIT) training: The provision of training only when it is needed to all but eliminate the loss of knowledge and skill caused by a lag between training and use.

K

Kaizen: A Japanese term that means gradual unending improvement by doing little things better and setting and achieving increasingly higher standards.

Kanban: A Japanese term for one of the primary tools of a just-in- time system. It maintains an orderly and efficient flow of materials throughout the entire manufacturing process. It is usually a printed card that contains specific information such as part name, description and quantity.

Key performance indicator (KPI): A statistical measure of how well an organization is doing in a particular area. A KPI could measure a company's financial performance or how it is holding up against customer requirements.

L

Leadership: An essential part of a quality improvement effort. Organization leaders must establish a vision, communicate that vision to those in the organization and provide the tools and knowledge necessary to accomplish the vision.

Lean: Producing the maximum sellable products or services at the lowest operational cost while optimizing inventory levels.

Lean enterprise: A manufacturing company organized to eliminate all unproductive effort and unnecessary investment, both on the shop floor and in office functions.

Lean manufacturing/production: An initiative focused on eliminating all waste in manufacturing processes. Principles of lean manufacturing include zero waiting time, zero inventory, scheduling (internal customer pull instead of push system), batch to flow (cut batch sizes), line balancing and cutting actual process times. The production systems are characterized by optimum automation, just-in-time supplier delivery disciplines, quick changeover times, high levels of quality and continuous improvement.

Lean migration: The journey from traditional manufacturing methods to one in which all forms of waste are systematically eliminated.

M

Master Black Belt (MBB): Lean Six Sigma or quality expert responsible for strategic implementations in an organization. An MBB is qualified to teach other Six Sigma facilitators the methods, tools and applications in all functions and levels of the company and is a resource for using statistical process control in processes.

Mean: The sum of the values divided by the number of values.

Measurement Systems Analysis: A method for evaluating how much variation occurs in the process by which we collect data, how accurate and reliable the process is for collecting data, and leverages the data collection plan to obtain measurements.

Mistake proofing: Use of production or design features to prevent the manufacture or passing downstream a nonconforming product; also known as "error proofing."

Muda: Japanese for waste; any activity that consumes resources but creates no value for the customer.

N

Non-value added: A term that describes a process step or function that is not required for the direct achievement of process output. This step or function is identified and examined for potential elimination. Also see "value added."

O

One-piece flow: The opposite of batch and queue; instead of building many products and then holding them in line for the next step in the process, products go through each step in the process one at a time, without interruption. Meant to improve quality and lower costs.

One-touch exchange of dies: The reduction of die setup to a single step. Also see "single-minute exchange of dies," "internal setup" and "external setup."

Overall equipment effectiveness (OEE): The product of a machine's operational availability, performance efficiency and first-pass yield.

Out-of-control process: A process in which the statistical measure being evaluated is not in a state of statistical control. In other words, the variations among the observed sampling results can be attributed to a constant system of chance causes. Also see "in-control process."

Outputs: Products, materials, services or information provided to customers (internal or external), from a process.

P

Pareto chart: A graphical tool for ranking causes from most significant to least significant. It is based on the Pareto principle, which was first defined by Joseph M. Juran in 1950. The principle, named after 19th century economist Vilfredo Pareto, suggests most effects come from relatively few causes; that is, 80% of the effects come from 20% of the possible causes. One of the "seven tools of quality" (see listing).

Plan-do-check-act (PDCA) cycle: A four-step process for quality improvement. In the first step (plan), a way to effect improvement is developed. In the second step (do), the plan is carried out, preferably on a small scale. In the third step (check), a study takes place between what was predicted and what was observed in the previous step. In the last step (act), action is taken on the causal system to effect the desired change. The plan-do-check-act cycle is sometimes referred to as the Shewhart cycle, because Walter A. Shewhart discussed the concept in his book Statistical Method From the Viewpoint of Quality Control, and as the Deming cycle, because W. Edwards Deming introduced the concept in Japan. The Japanese subsequently called it the Deming cycle. Also called the plan-do-study-act (PDSA) cycle.

Poka-yoke: Japanese term that means mistake proofing. A pokayoke device is one that prevents incorrect parts from being made or assembled or easily identifies a flaw or error.

Policy: An overarching plan (direction) for achieving an organization's goals.

Policy deployment: The selection of goals and projects to achieve the goals, designation of people and resources for project completion and establishment of project metrics.

Precision: The aspect of measurement that addresses repeatability or consistency when an identical item is measured several times.

Preventive action: Action taken to remove or improve a process to prevent potential future occurrences of a nonconformance.

Primary Metric: The primary measurement of the process in terms of output characteristics, traditionally correlated to time to deliver, cost, and quality.

Procedure: The steps in a process and how these steps are to be performed for the process to fulfill a customer's requirements; usually documented.

Process: A set of interrelated work activities characterized by a set of specific inputs and value added tasks that make up a procedure for a set of specific outputs.

Process capability: A statistical measure of the inherent process variability of a given characteristic. The most widely accepted formula for process capability is 6 sigma.

Process capability index: The value of the tolerance specified for the characteristic divided by the process capability. The several types of process capability indexes include the widely used Cpk and Cp.

Process improvement: The application of the plan-do-check-act cycle (see listing) to processes to produce positive improvement and better meet the needs and expectations of customers.

Process management: The pertinent techniques and tools applied to a process to implement and improve process effectiveness, hold the gains and ensure process integrity in fulfilling customer requirements.

Process map: A type of flowchart depicting the steps in a process and identifying responsibility for each step and key measures.

Process owner: The person who coordinates the various functions and work activities at all levels of a process, has the authority or ability to make changes in the process as required and manages the entire process cycle to ensure performance effectiveness.

Process performance management (PPM): The overseeing of process instances to ensure their quality and timeliness; can also include proactive and reactive actions to ensure a good result.

Process quality: The value of percentage defective or of defects per hundred units in product from a given process. Note: The symbols "p" and "c" are commonly used to represent the true process average in fraction defective or defects per unit; and "100p" and "100c" the true process average in percentage defective or in defects per hundred units.

Process re-engineering: A strategy directed toward major rethinking and restructuring of a process; often referred to as the "clean sheet of paper" approach.

Project management: The application of knowledge, skills, tools and techniques to a broad range of activities to meet the requirements of a particular project.

Pull system: An alternative to scheduling individual processes, in which the customer process withdraws the items it needs from a supermarket (see listing) and the supplying process produces to replenish what was withdrawn; used to avoid push. Also see "kanban."

Q

Quality: A subjective term for which each person or sector has its own definition. In technical usage, quality can have two meanings: 1. the characteristics of a product or service that bear on its ability to satisfy stated or implied needs; 2. a product or service free of deficiencies. According to Joseph Juran, quality means "fitness for use;" according to Philip Crosby, it means "conformance to requirements."

Quality audit: A systematic, independent examination and review to determine whether quality activities and related results comply with plans and whether these plans are implemented effectively and are suitable to achieve the objectives.

Quality circle: A quality improvement or self-improvement study group composed of a small number of employees (10 or fewer) and their supervisor. Quality circles originated in Japan, where they are called quality control circles.

Quality engineering: The analysis of a manufacturing system at all stages to maximize the quality of the process itself and the products it produces. Quality Excellence for Suppliers of Telecommunications

R

Reengineering: A breakthrough approach for restructuring an entire organization and its processes.

Regression Testing: A method for building a model of a response variable as a function of predictor variables using simple linear regression (using one predictor) or multi variable linear regression (using more than one predictor).

Reliability: The probability of a product's performing its intended function under stated conditions without failure for a given period of time.

Repeatability: The variation in measurements obtained when one measurement device is used several times by the same person to measure the same characteristic on the same product.

Reproducibility: The variation in measurements made by different people using the same measuring device to measure the same characteristic on the same product.

Requirements: The ability of an item to perform a required function under stated conditions for a stated period of time.

Right size: Matching tooling and equipment to the job and space requirements of lean production. Right sizing is a process that challenges the complexity of equipment by examining how equipment fits into an overall vision for workflow through a factory. When possible, right sizing favors smaller, dedicated machines rather than large, multipurpose batch processing ones.

Right the first time: The concept that it is beneficial and more cost effective to take the necessary steps up front to ensure a product or service meets its requirements than to provide a product or service that will need rework or not meet customer needs. In other words, an organization should engage in defect prevention rather than defect detection.

Risk management: Using managerial resources to integrate risk identification, risk assessment, risk prioritization, development of risk handling strategies and mitigation of risk to acceptable levels.

Robustness: The condition of a product or process design that remains relatively stable, with a minimum of variation, even though factors that influence operations or usage, such as environment and wear, are constantly changing.

Root cause: A factor that caused a nonconformance and should be permanently eliminated through process improvement.

S

S Chart: A graphical chart that represents the sample mean of baseline process performance to show process variation.

Scorecard: An evaluation device, usually in the form of a questionnaire, that specifies the criteria customers will use to rate your business' performance in satisfying customer requirements.

Self-directed work team (SDWT): A type of team structure in which much of the decision making regarding how to handle the team's activities is controlled by the team members themselves.

Service level agreement: A formal agreement between an internal provider and an internal receiver (customer).

Simple Random Sampling: A simple technique of selecting random samples of defects from the general population of data and analyzing that data to a specific confidence level.

Single-minute exchange of dies: A series of techniques pioneered by Shigeo Shingo for changeovers of production machinery in less than 10 minutes. The long-term objective is always zero setup, in which changeovers are instantaneous and do not interfere in any way with continuous flow. Setup in a single minute is not required, but used as a reference (see "one-touch exchange of dies," "internal setup" and "external setup").

Single-piece flow: A process in which products proceed, one complete product at a time, through various operations in design, order taking and production without interruptions, backflows or scrap.

SIPOC diagram: A tool used by Six Sigma process improvement teams to identify all relevant elements (suppliers, inputs, process, outputs, customers) of a process improvement project before work begins.

Six Sigma: A method that provides organizations tools to improve the capability of their business processes. This increase in performance and decrease in process variation lead to defect reduction and improvement in profits, employee morale and quality of products or services. Six Sigma quality is a term generally used to indicate a process is well controlled (± 6 s from the centerline in a control chart).

Sponsor: The person who supports a team's plans, activities and outcomes.

Stages of team growth: Four stages that teams move through as they develop maturity: forming, storming, norming and performing.

Stakeholder: Any individual, group or organization that will have a significant impact on or will be significantly impacted by the quality of a specific product or service.

Standard: The metric, specification, gauge, statement, category, segment, grouping, behavior, event or physical product sample against which the outputs of a process are compared and declared acceptable or unacceptable.

Standard work: A precise description of each work activity, specifying cycle time, takt time, the work sequence of specific tasks and the minimum inventory of parts on hand needed to conduct the activity. All jobs are organized around human motion to create an efficient sequence without waste. Work organized in such a way is called standard(ized) work. The three elements that make up standard work are takt time, working sequence and standard in-process stock (see individual listings).

Standard work instructions: A lean manufacturing tool that enables operators to observe a production process with an understanding of how assembly tasks are to be performed. It ensures the quality level is understood and serves as an excellent training aid, enabling replacement or temporary individuals to easily adapt and perform the assembly operation.

Standardization: When policies and common procedures are used to manage processes throughout the system. Also, English translation of the Japanese word seiketsu, one of the Japanese 5S's (see listing) used for workplace organization.

Statistical process control (SPC): The application of statistical techniques to control a process; often used interchangeably with the term "statistical quality control."

Supplier: A source of materials, service or information input provided to a process.

T

Takt time: The rate of customer demand, takt time is calculated by dividing production time by the quantity of product the customer requires in that time. Takt is the heartbeat of a lean manufacturing system. Also see "cycle time."

Theory of constraints (TOC): A lean management philosophy that stresses removal of constraints to increase throughput while decreasing inventory and operating expenses. TOC's set of tools examines the entire system for continuous improvement. The current reality tree, conflict resolution diagram, future reality tree, prerequisite tree and transition tree are the five tools used in TOC's ongoing improvement process. Also called constraints management.

Top management commitment: Participation of the highest level officials in their organization's quality improvement efforts. Their participation includes establishing and serving on a quality committee, establishing quality policies and goals, deploying those goals to lower levels of the organization, providing the resources and training lower levels need to achieve the goals, participating in quality improvement teams, reviewing progress organization wide, recognizing those who have performed well and revising the current reward system to reflect the importance of achieving the quality goals.

Total productive maintenance (TPM): A series of methods, originally pioneered by Nippondenso (a member of the Toyota group), to ensure every machine in a production process is always able to perform its required tasks so production is never interrupted.

Toyota House of Quality (See House of Quality)

Toyota production system (TPS): The production system developed by Toyota Motor Corp. to provide best quality, lowest cost and shortest lead time through eliminating waste. TPS is based on two pillars: just-in-time and jidohka (see listings). TPS is maintained and improved through iterations of standardized work and kaizen (see listing.)

U

Unit: An object for which a measurement or observation can be made; commonly used in the sense of a "unit of product," the entity of product inspected to determine whether it is defective or nondefective.

V

Value: Any activity that the customer cares about, significantly changes the product or service, and is done right the first time.

Value added: A term used to describe activities that transform input into a customer (internal or external) usable output.

Value Added Flow Analysis: A standard analysis activity that looks at all activities within a process and determines whether the activities are value added or non-value added in the eyes of the customer.

Value stream: All activities, both value added and nonvalue added, required to bring a product from raw material state into the hands of the customer, bring a customer requirement from order to delivery and bring a design from concept to launch. Also see "information flow" and "hoshin planning."

Value stream mapping: A pencil and paper tool used in two stages. First, follow a product's production path from beginning to end and draw a visual representation of every process in the material and information flows. Second, draw a future state map of how value should flow. The most important map is the future state map.

Visual controls: Any devices that help operators quickly and accurately gauge production status at a glance. Progress indicators and problem indicators help assemblers see when production is ahead, behind or on schedule. They allow everyone to instantly see the group's performance and increase the sense of ownership in the area. Also see "andon board," "kanban," "production board," "painted floor" and "shadow board."

Voice of the customer: The expressed requirements and expectations of customers relative to products or services, as documented and disseminated to the providing organization's members.

W

Waste: Any activity that consumes resources and produces no added value to the product or service a customer receives. Also known as muda.

Work Cells: Arranges operations and people in a cell (U-Shaped, etc.)

Work in process: Items between machines or equipment waiting to be processed.

World-class quality: A term used to indicate a standard of excellence: best of the best.

X

Xbar Chart: A graphical representation of the sample standard deviation of the baseline process performance. Evaluate Xbar Chart for evidence of special causes.

Z

Zbench: A process capability score that represents the best the process could do is the process was centered and everything in the process was held as constant as possible.

Zero defects: A performance standard and method Philip B. Crosby developed; states that if people commit themselves to watching details and avoiding errors, they can move closer to the goal of zero defects.

Made in the USA
Columbia, SC
08 September 2018